A timely book—the ideal author—practical guidelines for sensitizing the church to the mind of the unchurched. Hats off to Lee Strobel for a job well done.

Max Lucado

"Must" reading for anyone who wants to know what has to be done to make the church functional in terms of its mission.

The book is going to have a lot of people talking.

Tony Campolo, Professor of Sociology, Eastern College

The very first step to take in reaching the unchurched is that you must first learn to think like them. Unfortunately, the longer you are a believer, the less you tend to think like an unbeliever.

Lee Strobel is one of the most creative, brilliant communicators in the church today. He understands the mind of the unchurched because he was one! A powerful guidebook that any church can use to be more effective in sharing the Good News in the 1990s.

Rick Warren, Pastor of Saddleback Church

Christians of the 1990s need to learn how to translate the Gospel—without transforming it—in order to reach the unchurched Harrys and Marys of our post-Christian culture. Lee Strobel's lively, practical book is a tremendous tool for equipping believers to better understand the heads and hearts of their secular friends, and to better articulate the timeless truths of Christ in concepts that connect in the 1990s.

Ellen Santilli Vaughn, co-author, with Charles Colson
The Body: Being Light in Darkness

In the midst of explaining Christianity to a seeker, did you ever wish that a bubble revealing his thoughts would appear above his head like in the comic pages? If you only knew his mindset, you could be so much more effective explaining what matters so deeply to you in ways that make sense to him. Now that *Inside the Mind of Unchurched Harry and Mary* is available, we all have access to the inside thoughts of those who are searching to find God.

Howard G. Hendricks, Chairman
Center for Christian Leadership
Distinguished Professor, Dallas Theological Seminary

Lee Strobel is the perfect brain surgeon to get inside the mind of "unchurched Harry" because that's where his mind once was, too. Plenty of practical down-to-earth help for Harrys and Marys—and those who want to help them.

Russell Chandler, author/speaker
Former religion writer, *The Los Angeles Times*

Intensely practical, fun to read, non-threatening, relevant, informative, down-to-earth, humorous—all of these describe Lee Strobel's superb new book. You'll be glad you read it. Be sure your pastor reads it too.
Gary Collins, Executive Director
The American Association of Christian Counselors

Lee Strobel knows whereof he speaks. Proof can be seen any were in the thousands of seekers crowding the Willow Creek Community Church.
Robert E. Coleman, Ph.D., Trinity Evangelical Divinity School

The old adage, "If you aim at nothing you'll probably hit it" does not apply to Lee Strobel. He's taking aim at people who, like himself, until relatively recently, are unchurched pagans. He explains what happened to him, how it happened to others, and how we can see it happen.
D. Stuart Briscoe, Senior Pastor of Elmbrook Church

America's churches, even the megachurches, have for two decades been overly dependent on transfer growth. Lee Strobel's amazingly insightful book now provides the insights we have needed to reach the unsaved.
C. Peter Wagner, Professor of Church Growth
Fuller Theological Seminary

Understanding who the modern American is, how he thinks, and how he responds is a challenge to those of us who are committed to touching him with the Good News of Jesus Christ. Through the past few years, Lee Strobel has sought to get into the mind and heart of people outside the scope of the kingdom and has come to understand who they are and what it means to reach them. This book will help all of us learn from one who has made it a point to keep the Gospel uncompromised and the methods culturally relevant.
Joseph M. Stowell, President, Moody Bible Institute

Lee Strobel has helped those inside the church look into the minds of those outside the church. Anyone who has become comfortable in the church should read this manuscript to understand why the unsaved and unchurched are uncomfortable when they come into the congregation of believers. The author has one hand firmly on the unsaved and the other hand firmly in the church—bridging the gap between the two with this book.
Elmer L. Towns, Liberty University

With great perception, Lee Strobel gives outstanding insights into the minds of the unchurched, the barriers to their faith, and how to better relate to them. An excellent tool for evangelism.
Bill Bright, Campus Crusade for Christ

INSIDE THE MIND OF UNCHURCHED HARRY & MARY

How to
Reach Friends
and Family
Who Avoid God
and the Church

LEE STROBEL

FOREWORD BY BILL HYBELS

ZONDERVAN™

GRAND RAPIDS, MICHIGAN 49530 USA

WILLOW
CREEK
RESOURCES

To my mother,
Lorena Strobel,
who never lost faith in me.

ZONDERVAN™

Inside the Mind of Unchurched Harry and Mary
Copyright © 1993 by Lee Strobel

Requests for information should be addressed to:
Zondervan, *Grand Rapids, Michigan 49530*

Library of Congress Cataloging-in-Publication Data

Strobel, Lee Patrick.
    Inside the mind of unchurched Harry / how to reach friends and family
who avoid God and the church / Lee Strobel
       p. cm.
    ISBN 0-310-37561-4 (pbk.)
    1. Evangelistic work.   2. Irreligion.   3. Strobel, Lee Patrick.   I. Title.
BV3793.S78   1993
269.'.2 — dc20   92–43193
                                                          CIP

All Scripture quotations, unless otherwise indicated, are taken from the *Holy Bible:
New International Version*®. NIV®. Copyright © 1973, 1978, 1984 by International
Bible Society. Used by permission of Zondervan. All rights reserved.

Edited by John Sloan

Printed in the United States of America

---

02 03 04 05 06 07 08 /DC/ 31 30 29 28 27 26 25 24 23 22 21 20

CONTENTS

FOREWORD

Lee Strobel is a modern-day miracle. His life, like the apostle Paul's, is a tall trophy of God's grace . . . and no one is quicker to set the record straight on that point than Lee himself.

Lee was the kind of man that the safe, self-absorbed, traditional church rails against. Competitive, profane, witty, opportunistic, and thoroughly pagan, Lee was the type of person that many pastors warn the sheep to steer clear of if they want to keep their wool white.

But Lee, like so many others in our world, had a softness under that protective veneer that made him a wonderful candidate for conversion. He treasures his wife and children; he is a hopelessly curious person; and, most important, he is a sucker for the truth.

Watching Lee come to faith in Christ and seeing the transformation of his values, relationships, and ambitions has been one of the most remarkable acts of God that I've ever witnessed.

Recently I sat in the congregation of Willow Creek Community Church while Lee gave one of the most compelling cases for the truth of Christianity that I had ever heard in sermon form. My heart was beating out of my chest! I was awestruck by the powerful way that God was using Lee but also overwhelmed by the thought of how many of the old Lee Strobels are living in subdivisions within easy driving distance of churches all over our land. In that private moment I worshiped God for being a part of a local church that not only has a concern for "Unchurched Harrys," as we call them at Willow Creek, but has a workable strategy to reach them. Then I yearned for more churches to become intentional about reaching seekers.

That's what this book is about—how individual Christians and their churches can strategically penetrate the unchurched culture. Read it at your own risk. Lee is a dangerous communicator. . . . If you doubt me, read on.

Bill Hybels
January 1993

ACKNOWLEDGMENTS

I'm glad you've paused to look over this page because it's an important part of the book to me. Without the assistance and encouragement of a lot of friends, colleagues, and family members, this book would never have been written.

Thanks first to my wife, Leslie, and children, Alison and Kyle, for their loving support during the writing process and for their optimism that I'd finish even when I doubted it.

Also, my deep appreciation goes to Mark Mittelberg, my close friend and partner in ministry, who shared from his rich reservoir of evangelism experiences and made insightful suggestions for improving the manuscript.

I am also indebted to Senior Pastor Bill Hybels and the elders of Willow Creek Community Church, particularly Russ Robinson; the Willow Creek Association, including John Pearson and Jim Mellado; and my assistant, Laura Daughtry.

In addition, I appreciate the way George Barna and George Gallup, Jr., have advanced the understanding of the unchurched through their excellent statistical research.

The editors at Zondervan Publishing House deserve much credit for prodding me to broaden my original vision for this project. Thanks especially to John Raymond and John Sloan, who played key roles in shaping the book and keeping it on track.

1
INTRODUCING YOU TO UNCHURCHED HARRY AND MARY

My wife, Leslie, and I were celebrating at an Italian restaurant across the street from the University of Missouri. I was set to graduate in a few days, and I had just accepted a job offer: a three-month internship at *The Chicago Tribune*, with a promise that if I performed well I'd get a permanent job as a reporter.

For a journalism junkie who grew up feasting on Chicago's four aggressive daily newspapers, it was a dream come true.

My best friend, Ersin, a Turkish-born student from a Muslim family, joined us for our impromptu party. At one point during the meal, somewhere between the bread sticks and the Neapolitan ice cream, he made an offhand remark about how my internship was certainly a great gift from God.

His comment startled me. During the four years I had known Ersin, religion had virtually never come up as a topic. "Wait a second, let me get this straight," I said. "Are you telling me that someone as intelligent as you—valedictorian, science whiz, pre-med student and all that—that you actually believe that God exists? I always figured you were beyond that!"

I was incredulous, but it was clear that Ersin was equally astonished. "What are you trying to tell *me*?" he said. "Are you saying there *isn't* a God? Are you telling me that someone as intelligent as you *doesn't* believe in God? You've got to be kidding! I always assumed that *everybody* believed in God."

We were both genuinely amazed by each other's position. For me, I couldn't believe that a sharp person like Ersin had actually bought into a fairy tale like the existence of an all-powerful, all-knowing Creator of the universe.

Hadn't he learned *anything* at college? Hadn't Darwin explained that life was merely an accident of evolution? Hadn't Marx established that religion was only a tool used by the powerful to oppress the poor? Hadn't Freud argued convincingly that religious beliefs are empty illusions that grow out of "the oldest, strongest and most urgent wishes of mankind," a desire for protection against the dangers of life?[1]

It seemed to me that thinking people just weren't the religious type. Oh, they may play the religion game, going to church from time to time because it's the socially acceptable thing to do. After all, what better place is there to meet potential business clients?

But deep down inside, they certainly weren't convinced that they had a great celestial Father, were they? Let's face it: If people *really* believed that, they'd be living their lives quite a bit differently.

If you could freeze-frame my attitude toward God, circa 1974, that would be it. Frankly, I thought the idea of God was pretty ridiculous. But then if you were to fast-forward the videotape of my life, zipping past a thirteen-year journalism career, you'd come upon an unlikely picture: a once-cynical and stone-hearted newspaperman preaching the Gospel at a large evangelical church.

An unlikely picture but a true reflection of what God has done. Today my life is dedicated to helping irreligious people— doubters as I once was—discover the life-changing and eternity-altering reality of Jesus Christ.

The transition from what I was in that Italian restaurant in Columbia, Missouri, to what I later became at Willow Creek Community Church in suburban Chicago is the story of one modern skeptic's journey to faith. And yet in a broader sense, it's also a story that parallels the spiritual pilgrimage of many people who have discovered Christ through the ministry of Willow Creek and similar churches.

You see, Willow Creek is a church that is geared for the unchurched. Ever since Bill Hybels and a core of friends started the ministry in a movie theater in 1975, they have focused their efforts on trying to reach non-Christians, whom they have affectionately nicknamed "Unchurched Harry" and "Unchurched Mary."

So who are Harry and Mary?

• Harry is the science teacher at the local high school who thinks that all religion is for intellectual weaklings.

• Mary is the extroverted neighbor who's perfectly happy without God in her life.

• Harry is the foreman at the construction site who uses Jesus' name only as a swear word.

• Mary is the entrepeneur who's so busy dealing with her success that she doesn't have time for spiritual matters.

• Harry is the businessman who shies away from Christianity because he's afraid it might cramp the way he conducts his business.

• Mary is the university student whose bitter experiences with her dad have poisoned her attitude toward the idea of a heavenly Father.

• Harry is the husband who thinks that his wife's faith is a waste of time.

• Mary is the dentist who does believe that Jesus Christ is

the Son of God, but she keeps putting off any kind of personal response to him.

• Harry is the auto mechanic who goes to church religiously—every Christmas and Easter, whether he needs it or not.

• Mary is the accountant who takes her children to church so that they can get some moral training, and though she sits through the services herself, in her heart she's really unchurched.

• Harry is the lawyer who spends his Sunday mornings leisurely reading the newspaper, or playing eighteen holes of golf at the country club—and he chafes at the idea that he should feel guilty about it.

• Mary is the government bureaucrat who was turned off to God by an early church experience that left her convinced that Christianity is at best boring and irrelevant, and at worst, a scam to bilk the naive.

Although this book is written from a male perspective, almost all of the advice will be useful in bringing the Gospel to women who have ignored or rejected God. So when I say "Harry" in this book, I am also saying, "Mary," since the basic principles apply to women as well as to men.

Over the years since I became a Christian, I've been kidded that I'm the quintessential Unchurched Harry. While there have been a lot of others, it's true that I did fit Unchurched Harry's profile. And maybe you know someone who does, too.

Maybe you have a colleague at work, a neighbor down the block, a friend that you play tennis with, or even a spouse who's indifferent or skeptical toward Christianity. You desperately want God to use you to bring the Gospel to that individual, but you're not sure what to do.

Or maybe you're entering the ministry and are anxious to penetrate your community with the message of Christ, but you're afraid you might scare off more people than you reach.

Or perhaps you're already a church leader, and you're frustrated because your congregation seems to be in the business of merely re-energizing wayward Christians. You want to reach *real* irreligious people, and yet you're not sure how you and your church can effectively connect with them.

Part of your hesitation in proceeding might stem from your own uncertainties about Unchurched Harry and Mary. You may wonder whether you really understand them well enough to know how to lovingly, tactfully, and powerfully bring them the Gospel. After all, it may have been quite a while since you've lived a secular lifestyle—if you've ever lived one at all.

You may have found that since you've become a Christian, your unbelieving friends have drifted away as you've become increasingly involved in the social network of the church. It has been said that within two years of becoming a Christian, the average person has already lost the significant relationships he once had with people outside the faith.[2] Without frequent heart-to-heart conversations with unchurched people, it's easy to forget how they think.

That's why I wrote this book: to help advance your understanding of unchurched people so that your personal evangelistic efforts and the efforts of your church might become more effective.

That's my goal because, frankly, I love irreligious people. Some of my best friends are, in reality, hell-bound pagans, and I am impassioned about wanting to see them transformed by the same amazing grace that radically redirected the trajectory of my own life.

I'm sure that you feel the same way about people you know. I don't think you're reading this book because it has a catchy title or because you've ever heard of me. You're reading it because you're hungry to see your friends and relatives adopted into God's family and, hopefully, to see your entire community impacted by the Gospel. Hey, we share the same goals, so let's team up!

I'll do my part by tapping into my personal experiences and what I've learned in leading irreligious people to Christ. Then you do your part by taking what you think might be helpful for your situation, discarding the rest, and then following God's leadings as he dispatches you on your next adventure in evangelism.

Let me concede up front that I'm not a psychologist, social scientist, or public opinion researcher. All of those experts can offer important insights into why people reject God and the church, and I'll be citing some of their findings in this book. But while I may not be an academic expert, I'll tell you this: *I was radically rescued from an aimless life of atheism, and those years of living apart from God left an indelible imprint on me.*

That experience is still fresh enough in my mind to help me empathize with what's aching inside the thousands of unchurched people whom I've addressed at outreach services and events. And it's my hope that what I've experienced as an unbeliever, as well as what I've learned as an evangelist to skeptics, will help you sharpen your own evangelistic edge, regardless of whether you're part of a traditional or contemporary church.

Let me emphasize that I'm not proud of the life I led before I came to Christ. In fact, I wish I had committed my life to the Lord long before the age of thirty. I would have avoided a lot of pain for myself and others.

But one of the most hope-packed verses in Scripture says, "And we know that in all things God works for the good of those who love him, who have been called according to his purpose."[3]

Sometimes when I read that promise from God, I think: *Can any good come out of the raw, turbulent years I spent as Unchurched Harry?* And yet, wouldn't it be just like God to answer yes? Wouldn't it be just like Him to create something positive out of that admittedly profane and sinful era of my life?

God can do that. He can actually take my experience of living apart from Him and use it to help you, and I understand how we can reach out to irreligious people who don't even realize that they need God. That's what I pray will be the end result of this book—for the sake of all the Unchurched Harrys and Marys.

2

HARRY'S JOURNEY BEGINS

"Unchurched Harry."

Sure, I've been kidded that I was Unchurched Harry, but actually that's too mild a nickname to describe my attitude back then. It sounds like someone who's stuck in spiritual neutral. A more appropriate description of my mindset would have been "Anti-Church Charlie" because I was so negative toward spiritual matters.

For most of my adult life, I considered myself an atheist. Admittedly, I hadn't analyzed the evidence for and against the existence of God before I concluded that He didn't exist. I merely thought the concept of an almighty deity was absurd on its surface.

Why devote time to checking out such obvious wishful thinking? Angels and demons—come on! It did not take much of a dose of modern science to debunk the Sunday school mythology of my childhood.

Even as a youngster, I was the skeptical sort. When I'd go into an ice-cream shop, I'd count all the flavors just to make sure there were thirty-one like the sign said. I was the kind of high school student who peppered teachers with remarks like, "Prove it to me," and "How do you know?" So I suppose it was natural for me to pursue journalism as a career. It seemed like the perfect profession for an iconoclast who liked to write.

From an early age, I was fascinated by newspapers. I loved to read *The Chicago Tribune* before breakfast and *The Chicago Daily News* after dinner because they were aggressive and tough-minded. They seemed to subscribe to the old axiom that newspapers exist to comfort the afflicted and afflict the comfortable. I wanted that to be my motto, too.

When I was eleven years old, I started a neighborhood newspaper called *The Arlington Bulletin* in my hometown of Arlington Heights, Illinois, a suburb northwest of Chicago. With the help of some buddies, I produced the five-page *Bulletin* on a decrepit mimeograph machine every week for two years, publishing everything from local crime stories and politics to reports on new residents of the area.

At one point, Stanton Cook, then production manager of *The Chicago Tribune*, got wind of our paper, and he came over to see my "newsroom" in our basement. When a *Tribune* reporter later interviewed me for an article, I was able to articulate a firm vision of my future: I wanted to get my degree from the University of Missouri's journalism school and then embark on a career in Chicago, one of the country's most tumultuous newspaper towns.

GRADUATING FROM CHURCH

I wasn't concerned much about spiritual issues as a child. My parents certainly encouraged me to believe in God, and they brought me and my four brothers and sisters to a Lutheran church on a regular basis. Frankly, I hated it, and so periodically

I'd fake a sore throat and say that I was too sick to go. Of course, my mom would reply, "If you're too sick for church, then you're too sick to go outside and play this afternoon." That usually cured me.

What I recall most from Sunday school is the mind-numbing boredom of it all. I vaguely remember a jumble of stories about men who wore robes and rode camels, people I just couldn't relate to. It was worse when I'd go to the adult service; the twenty-minute sermons seemed interminable, and the whole time I was supposed to sit still and be quiet. I don't remember much of the content other than some talk about Jesus' dying on the cross and paying for our sins, but I never could quite comprehend the connection between the two.

All the kids in our family were expected to go through the church's confirmation process. That meant going to church for religious training for a few hours each week during parts of seventh and eighth grades.

We would sit in a strict classroom while the pastor tried to stuff theology into our uncooperative heads. Each week the class was assigned a chunk of the catechism to memorize, such as one of the Ten Commandments and the commentary on it. Of course, I never studied the assignment until I was walking to church the next week and so I would sit in the back row with sweaty palms until I'd have to stand and fumble my way through the recital.

The pastor seemed exasperated by the attitude of much of the class. And, to be honest, we were a pretty exasperating bunch. I still remember his favorite word: "diligence." I wasn't sure what it meant; all I knew was that we sure didn't have much of it. Believe me, he made *that* clear.

In eighth grade, we were presented to the church. Beforehand, the pastor drilled us on the kind of questions that he was going to ask, and when we stood before the congregation, we said what we had been taught to say. I really can't remember much about it.

In some ways, though, it was like graduation, because not only did we graduate from the confirmation process but we also graduated from church. At least, I did. Now that I had done the "religion thing" by being confirmed, the decision of whether to go to church was pretty much left up to me. Basically, I felt liberated from my religious commitment except for Christmas and Easter.

THE *OTHER* WOODSTOCK

All of which freed me to live the way I wanted to. Although I maintained the facade of being an all-American boy, this was the late '60s, when the sexual revolution was in full swing, and I was an eager participant. There were times when I'd also supply liquor to high school students in the area. Some of it I'd steal from my dad's supply that he kept in our basement, selling it for three dollars a bottle for gin and five dollars a bottle for *Early Times*. I didn't drink it myself, although I certainly made up for that later in life. While in high school, I was just in it for the cash.

After my sophomore, junior, and senior years of high school, I moved away from home as soon as the school year ended and lived in a boarding house or apartment in Woodstock, Illinois, which was about twenty-five miles away. I spent the summers working as a reporter and photographer for the *Woodstock Daily Sentinel*.

As a result, I learned a lot about journalism, but I also learned a great deal about life. I was supporting myself on my eighty dollars-a-week salary (my room at the boarding house was only fifteen dollars a week), and I enjoyed the freedom of living without adult oversight. My roommate brewed raisin wine in the closet, and I was always out trying to meet girls to bring over to our place. The summers in Woodstock were pretty wild.

But as far as girlfriends were concerned, there was only one I really loved. Her name was Leslie Hirdler, and we met when we were fourteen years old. On the same day that a mutual friend introduced us, Leslie went home and said to her mother, "I've met the boy I'm going to marry."

Her mother was quite condescending. "Sure, you did," she said. But Leslie didn't have any doubts, and neither did I.

We dated on and off during high school, and after I left home to attend the University of Missouri, we maintained our relationship through the mail. We became convinced that there was nobody else we would ever be happy with. Within a year, Leslie moved down to Missouri, and we got engaged. We decided to get married in a church because, well, that's where people get married, isn't it?

Besides, Leslie wasn't as hostile toward spiritual matters as I was. I suppose you would describe her as being spiritually ambivalent. When she was a youngster, her parents took her to a Methodist church for a while. Later, she occasionally attended a Presbyterian church with her Scottish mother, and she remembers her mom softly singing hymns to her when being put to bed as a little girl.

But for Leslie, the topic of God was largely a curiosity she had never taken the time to seriously explore.

LIVING IN HIGH GEAR

At the end of my senior year in college, I was getting ready to graduate and was weighing job prospects around the country. My ultimate goal was still to work in Chicago, but I hadn't applied there because of the tight market. Then one day a professor said, "I got a call from *The Chicago Tribune*. They want to interview you for an internship."

I was stunned. The *Tribune* was calling for me? What I didn't know at the time was that Stanton Cook, the *Tribune*'s production manager who had been so impressed with the *Arlington Bulletin* when I was a kid, had been promoted to publisher of the *Tribune* in the intervening years. He remembered my passion for journalism, and he suggested that the editors check me out.

The result was that I accepted a three-month internship as sort of a trial run—and after proving myself for six weeks, I was promoted to full-fledged general assignment reporter.

That's when my life power-shifted into high gear. In fact, if I had a god at the time, it was my career. I enjoyed having a front-row seat to history, covering everything from gangland murders to major fires to labor strikes to political controversies. I was butting heads with some of the journalistic legends whose bylines I had grown up reading.

And my own byline began to make regular appearances on the front page of the *Tribune*. In fact, one day I had three front-page stories. I loved seeing my name in print, and I thrived on the cutthroat environment, the adrenaline rush of deadlines, and the get-the-story-at-any cost mentality.

I was known as an aggressive and accurate reporter. There were times, however, when I went over the ethical edge, like when I'd call crime victims and witnesses from the press room at the police department and identify myself by saying, "This is Lee Strobel calling from police headquarters." Technically, that was true, but actually it was a ploy to mislead people into thinking they were talking to a cop instead of a reporter. After all, people will tell the police a great deal more than they'll tell a journalist.

And when I was on the heels of a hot story and needed some documents from U.S. District Court, I would stuff the papers under my coat and steal them—a federal crime—so that my competitors couldn't find them. After my article hit the streets, I'd return the papers to their file. My attitude was that ethics were fine to discuss in journalism school, but they shouldn't get in the way of getting a good story.

Over time I was promoted to covering criminal courts and for two years was immersed in a daily world of murder, rape, and assault cases. Later, I was assigned to the more prestigious federal-court beat, where I covered a better breed of criminal, including crooked politicians, corrupt union bosses, unscrupulous business executives, and organized-crime racketeers. Since I was intrigued by legal issues and trials, I took time out to earn a master's degree at Yale Law School, returning to the *Tribune* as legal-affairs editor.

I was doing what I had always dreamed of: traveling around the country; covering major trials, court decisions, and legal trends; doing radio and TV interview shows; writing a book; winning awards. I had *made* it. I was on the fast track to the top of my profession, and I wasn't even thirty years old.

DEVELOPING HEART DISEASE

Looking back, I can see how I had been intoxicated by the power of the press. Sure, there were times when I used it for good. I remember doing a Thanksgiving Day feature about the Delgados, a poverty-stricken family on Chicago's West Side. The two young sisters were too poor to own a coat and had only one sweater between them. During the biting Chicago winter, one would wear the sweater halfway to school, the other would wear it the remainder of the distance.

After my article appeared, big-hearted people from around the city showered them with gifts and money. I went back to visit them on Christmas Eve and found their home overflowing with presents—and their closet so stuffed that it looked like the coat department at Marshall Field's. It was a good lesson on how the media can help people in need.

But to be honest, what I really savored was making big shots dance to the newspaper's tune. I gloated when one of the most powerful politicians in Chicago called to literally beg me not to run a story that was going to damage his re-election chances. "Fat chance," I said. "Remember the time you leaked that story about the Sam Giancana murder case to Mike Royko instead of me? Well, it's pay-back time."

I barked snide questions at the Illinois Attorney General

after he emerged from a grand jury that was investigating him. As he squeezed past me in the hall, he snarled, "You think you know all the answers, don't you, Strobel?" I shot back, "What are you trying to hide, you crook?"

I remember waiting until Thanksgiving to call a wealthy businessman so that I could interrupt his cheerful holiday celebration by saying, "I'm printing a story in tomorrow's paper that you're under investigation for fraud. Do you have any comment?"

Once a major corporation flew in several executives to try to convince the *Tribune* to back off from an editorial we were planning in connection with a series of articles I was writing. "You're wasting your time," I told them. "Nothing you say is going to stop us."

It was heady stuff. Being a big-city newspaperman can be an ego trip; it stoked mine to the limit.

But after a while, I began to notice that I was becoming increasingly desensitized to other people. I recall interviewing a grieving woman whose young daughter had been raped and murdered. As she poured out her pain, I remember thinking to myself, "Wow! These are great quotes! And I'm the only reporter who's got them!" I didn't care about her daughter or her despair; I was after a front-page byline and another bonus from the boss.

Even other people noticed my hardening heart. Once I covered a trial in which the key witness was a teenage gang member. He testified how a rival gang had lined up him and his friends against a wall and then, one by one, shot them point-blank in the head. Three of his friends died instantly; somehow, he survived. At least, he survived long enough to point out the killers in court. According to a doctor's testimony, it was only a matter of time before the witness himself would probably die from his injuries.

After the trial was over, the prosecutor allowed me to interview the teenager for a feature story. I was excited because I knew it was going to be a front-page exclusive. In fact, I was so pumped-up about beating the competition to the story that I was interviewing the witness in a very lighthearted and upbeat way.

In the middle of the interview, the prosecutor pulled me aside and said angrily, "Strobel, what's wrong with you? This kid watched three of his friends get blown away, he's probably going to die himself, and you're interviewing him like you're Bob Hope or something."

His words haunted me for a long time. What *was* wrong with me? Why didn't I care about that kid or his murdered friends? Why did I not empathize with the woman whose daughter had been murdered? Why did I only care about myself, my byline, and my career?

The Bible has a term for it—hardness of heart.

A CHURCH FOR THE UNCHURCHED

By 1979, Leslie and I were living in Arlington Heights with our two children, Alison and Kyle. During this time, Leslie became close friends with a woman named Linda Lenssen whose daughter, Sara, was the same age as Alison.

Linda, as it turned out, was a Christian, and as her relationship with Leslie deepened, she began to share her faith with her. Leslie was receptive, especially because she saw congruence between the beliefs that Linda professed and the kind of life that Linda was leading.

But soon Linda found herself in a quandary. She had already explained the Gospel to Leslie and tried to answer her questions, and while she sensed God's working in Leslie's life, she didn't know what to do next. Almost instinctively, though, she knew what *not* to do.

She knew that she risked doing more harm than good if she were to bring Leslie to her church for a Sunday service. Though Linda attended a solid Bible-believing fellowship, she knew that Leslie wouldn't connect with its traditional approach.

She would be baffled by the Christian lingo, she'd find the

music oddly outdated, and the sermon would be intended for Christians and would probably leave her confused. Besides, all the church offered was a worship service, and Leslie wasn't ready to worship God. She was still trying to figure out who He was.

That's when Linda saw a newspaper article about a different kind of church that was meeting in the Willow Creek Theater, less than a mile from our home. The article called it a contemporary church that was trying to be relevant to people who were investigating the Christian faith. It sounded like a good partner to team up with in trying to bring Leslie to a point of decision.

One day Linda nervously took the step of inviting Leslie to Willow Creek. "I read an article about a new kind of church that's meeting in a movie theater," she said. "Jerry and I were thinking of going to see what it's like. Want to come along?" She held her breath as Leslie thought about it.

"Well, I don't know," Leslie replied.

She was too polite to say what she was really thinking: "It's okay to talk about God with you, but going to a church, well, I'm just not sure. The church I remember as a child was so intimidating. I'm not sure how to behave. Or how to dress. Or what to say. Or when to stand up and sit down. Or how to look up a verse in the Bible. Will the pastor pressure me into making a decision about something that I'm not ready to make? What if these people are Jesus freaks? What if it's some sort of cult?"

CONNECTING WITH GOD

But by the time Sunday rolled around, Leslie's curiosity got the best of her, and she agreed to go. To her surprise, she loved it. She came home and excitedly told me about the great music, the poignant drama, the clever multi-media, and the sermon by a guy our age who seemed to be talking our language.

Of course, I wasn't interested. In fact, I remember asking, "You didn't give those guys any of our money, did you?" Despite my attitude, Leslie kept going with the Lenssens every Sunday. She found that the messages provided great grist for the ongoing spiritual conversations she was having with Linda.

Leslie kept asking questions, kept seeking after the truth, until finally, in September 1979, she came up to me and said: "Lee, I've made a big decision. I've decided to follow Jesus Christ."

I have to admit that I was about as condescending as her mother was when Leslie told her at age fourteen that she had met the person she was going to marry. "If you think that's going to make you a better person, then that's okay with me," I said, "but don't try to get me involved!"

Leslie's conversion actually ended up sparking the most tumultuous era in our marriage, as I'll describe in Chapter 9. It turned out that Leslie did keep encouraging me to go, and I kept resisting. After all, what did I need church for? I was a success in my career, had a house in the suburbs, a wife and two kids, a nice car—who needed God? Besides, to me, church was four things: boring, hypocritical, money-grubbing, and irrelevant.

Yet, over the next couple of months, I started to sense subtle changes in Leslie's character as the Holy Spirit began to change her. I'm not saying that she turned into Mother Teresa overnight, but there was a definite blossoming of her personality.

I detected it in the way she related to the children. I saw it in her more loving demeanor toward me and others. I watched her develop more self-confidence and patience. Those changes, combined with her insistence that I would love the music, convinced me in January 1980 to venture inside Willow Creek for the first time.

ACCEPTING THE CHALLENGE

Leslie was right—I did like the music. Instead of an organ wheezing tired old hymns, the songs were a kind of driving soft-rock, and I thought they were great in spite of the Christian lyrics. I liked the dramas and multi-media, too, and the fact that the place seemed alive with electricity. But most of all I was captivated by the message.

It was delivered by Bill Hybels, who was my age and who stood before the audience without notes or a lectern. He dressed like a young businessman, and instead of railing at us, he spoke in a sincere conversational tone, like a friend talking to a friend.

"What does God say it will take for life to have purpose, direction, and meaning in a fallen society?" he asked. "What does it take to have a transformation of the heart?"

My mind flashed to the condition of my own heart as I recalled that prosecutor's stinging words: *Strobel, what's wrong with you?* Hybels had my attention.

He used an overhead projector to draw a graphic depiction of the "popular perception" about Christianity, and then he critiqued it from a biblical perspective. He explained that because of Christ's love for us He willingly died on the cross as our substitute so we wouldn't have to pay for our own wrongdoing. For the first time, the connection between the Cross and my own life became clear.

At the end, he issued two challenges. For those who were ready, he urged them to receive Christ's free gift of forgiveness and His leadership of their life. For those who weren't, he encouraged them to continue checking out the claims of Christianity.

I was intrigued by both the message and his concession that some people needed to go through a discovery process before they could make an informed decision about Christ. While I didn't believe the Gospel was true, he had convinced me that if it were the truth, it had tremendous implications for my life.

So as I walked out of the theater that morning into the brisk air, I made a decision. I vowed to check out the Christian faith. I'd separate mythology from reality and see what remained. After all, that's what I did every day as a journalist—I'd take a nugget of information and investigate to see whether it's true.

Why not put Christianity to the same test?

3

A SKEPTIC'S
SURPRISE

For a person who considered himself an atheist, I embarked on my spiritual journey in an unusual way.

I asked God for help.

I figured, what's the downside? If I'm right and nobody's at home in heaven, then all I've lost is thirty seconds. If I'm wrong and God is listening—well, there could be a big upside. So in the privacy of my room on January 20, 1980, I prayed along these lines:

God, I don't even believe You're there, but if You are, I want to find You. I really do want to know the truth. So if You exist, please show Yourself to me.

What I didn't know at the time was that this simple prayer would launch me on a nearly two-year adventure of discovery that would end up revolutionizing my life.

Using my legal training, which gave me knowledge about

evidence, and my journalism background, which gave me skills in ferreting out facts, I began to read books and interview experts. I was greatly influenced by Josh McDowell, whose books *More Than a Carpenter*[1] and *Evidence That Demands a Verdict*[2] first opened my eyes to the possibility that a person could have an intellectually defensible faith.

Of course, I also read the Bible. However, for the moment I set aside the issue of whether it really was the inspired word of God. Instead, I took the Bible for what it undeniably is—a collection of ancient documents purporting to record historical events.

I also read other religious writings, including the Book of Mormon, because I thought it important to check out different spiritual options. Most of them were easy to dismiss. For instance, Mormonism quickly fell by the wayside after I found irreconcilable discrepancies between the claims of its founder, Joseph Smith, and the findings of modern archaeology. But with Christianity, the more I found out, the more intrigued I became.

I visualized this process as if I were putting together a giant jigsaw puzzle in my mind. Every time I confirmed another item of evidence or a question was answered, it was like a puzzle piece being put into place. I didn't know what the final picture was going to look like—that was the mystery—but each fact I uncovered brought me one step closer to the solution.

ANSWERS FOR AN ATHEIST

Right off the bat, I figured that Christians had made a tactical error. Other religions believe in all kinds of amorphous, invisible gods, and that's kind of hard to pin down one way or the other. But Christians were basing their religion on the alleged teachings and miracles of someone they claimed is an actual historical person—Jesus Christ—who, they said, is God.

I thought this a major mistake because if Jesus really lived, He would have left behind some historical evidence. I figured that all I needed to do was ascertain the historical truth about Jesus and I would find that He was a nice man, maybe a very moral person and excellent teacher, but certainly nothing at all like a god.

I began by asking myself the first question any good journalist asks: "How many eyeballs are there?" The term "eyeball" is slang for eyewitness. Everyone knows how convincing eyewitness testimony can be in establishing the veracity of an event. Believe me, I've seen plenty of defendants sent to prison by eyewitnesses.

So I wanted to know, "How many witnesses met this person named Jesus? How many heard His teachings? How many watched Him perform miracles? How many actually saw Him after he supposedly returned from the dead?"

I was surprised to discover that there wasn't just a single eyewitness; there were many, and the New Testament contains actual writings by several of them. For instance, there are Matthew, Peter, John, and James—they were all eyewitnesses. There's the historian Mark, who recorded Peter's firsthand account; there's Luke, a physician who wrote a biography of Jesus based on eyewitness testimony; and there's Paul, whose life was turned upside down after he said he had encountered the resurrected Christ.

Peter was adamant that he was accurately recording firsthand information. "We did not follow cleverly invented stories when we told you about the power and coming of our Lord Jesus Christ," he wrote, "but we were eyewitnesses of his majesty."[3]

John said he was writing about things "which we have heard, which we have seen with our eyes, which we have looked at and our hands have touched."[4]

TRUSTWORTHY TESTIMONY

Not only were these people eyewitnesses, but, McDowell pointed out, they were preaching about Jesus to people who had lived at the same time and in the same area that Jesus did. This is important because if the disciples were exaggerating or rewriting history, their often-hostile audiences would have known it and thrown them out. But instead, they were able to talk about matters that were common knowledge to their audiences.[5]

For instance, shortly after Jesus was killed, Peter spoke to a crowd in the same city where the Crucifixion had taken place. Many of them probably had seen Jesus put to death. He started out by saying: "Men of Israel, listen to this: Jesus of Nazareth was a man accredited by God to you by miracles, wonders and signs, which God did among you through him, *as you yourselves know*."[6]

In other words, "C'mon, everybody—you know what Jesus did. You saw these things for yourself!" Then he pointed out that although King David was dead and still in his tomb, "God has raised this Jesus to life, and we are all witnesses of the fact."[7]

The audience's reaction was very interesting. They didn't say, "We don't know what you're talking about!" Instead, they panicked and wanted to know what they should do. On that day about three thousand people sought forgiveness and many others followed—apparently because they knew that Peter was telling the truth.[8]

I had to ask myself, "Would Christianity have taken root as quickly as it undeniably did if these disciples were going around saying things that their audiences knew were exaggerated or false?"

Jigsaw pieces began fitting into place.

One bit of evidence that Christians were trying to sell me— and which I wasn't buying—was that Jesus' disciples must have believed what they were preaching about Him because ten of the eleven remaining disciples suffered terrible deaths rather than recant their testimony that Jesus was the Son of God who had risen from the dead. Several were tortured to death through crucifixion.

At first, I didn't find that persuasive. I could point to all sorts of crackpots through history who were willing to die for their religious beliefs. But the disciples were different, McDowell said. People will die for their religious beliefs if they are convinced that their beliefs are true, but people won't die for their religious beliefs if they know their beliefs are false.

In other words, the whole Christian faith hinges on whether Jesus Christ actually rose from the dead.[9] No resurrection, no Christianity. The disciples said that they saw Jesus after He rose from the dead. They knew whether or not they were lying; there was no way this could have been a hallucination or mistake. And if they were lying, would they willingly allow themselves to be killed for what they knew to be false?

As McDowell observed, *Nobody knowingly and willingly dies for a lie.*[10]

That single fact had a powerful influence on me, even more so when I looked at what happened to the disciples after the Crucifixion. History shows that they went out to boldly proclaim that Jesus overcame the tomb. Suddenly, these once-cowardly men are filled with courage, willing to preach to their death that Jesus was the Son of God.

What transformed them? I couldn't come up with an explanation that made more sense than that they really did have a life-changing experience with the resurrected Christ.

A FIRST-CENTURY SKEPTIC

I came to especially like the disciple named Thomas because he was as skeptical as I was. I figured he would have made a great journalist. Thomas said he wasn't going to believe that Jesus had returned to life unless he could personally examine the wounds in Jesus' hands and feet.

According to the New Testament records, Jesus did appear and invite Thomas to check out the evidence for himself, and Thomas saw that it was true. I was fascinated to find out how he spent the rest of his life. According to tradition, he ended up proclaiming—until he was stabbed to death in India—that Jesus was the Son of God who had returned from the dead. For him, the evidence had been profoundly convincing.

Also, it was significant to read what Thomas said after becoming satisfied by the evidence that Jesus had overcome death. Thomas proclaimed: "My Lord and my God!"[11]

Now, Jesus didn't respond by saying, "Whoa! Wait a minute, Tom. Don't go worshiping me. You should only worship God, and remember, I'm just a great teacher and a very moral man." Instead, Jesus accepted Thomas' worship.

So it didn't take long to disprove the popular conception that Jesus never claimed He was God. For years, skeptics had been telling me that Jesus never pretended that He was anything more than a man and that He'd roll over in His grave if He knew that people were worshiping Him. But as I read the Bible, I found Jesus affirming over and over again—through word and deed—who He really was.

Christ's oldest biography describes how He was asked point-blank by the high priest during his trial: "Are you the Christ, the Son of the Blessed One?"[12] Jesus wasn't ambiguous. The first two words out of His mouth were: "I am."[13]

The high priest knew what Jesus was saying, because He angrily declared to the court, "You have heard the blasphemy."[14] What was blasphemous? That Jesus was claiming to be God! This, I learned, is the crime for which He was put to death.

As I was becoming more confident in the New Testament's eyewitness accounts, I kept remembering what other skeptics had told me through the years. They claimed that the New Testament couldn't be trusted because it was written a hundred or more years after Jesus lived. They said that myths about Jesus had grown up during the interim and distorted the truth beyond recognition.

But as I assessed the facts with fairness, I found out that recent archaeological discoveries have forced scholars to give earlier and earlier estimates for when the New Testament was written.

Dr. William Albright, a world-renowned professor from Johns Hopkins University and former director of the American School of Oriental Research in Jerusalem, said he's convinced that the various books of the New Testament were written within fifty years after the Crucifixion and very probably within twenty and forty-five years of Jesus' death.[15] This means that the New Testament was available during the lifetimes of eyewitnesses who would have disputed its contents if they had been fabricated.

What's more, scholars have studied the amount of time it took for legend to develop in the ancient world. Their conclusion: There would not have been anywhere near enough time between the death of Jesus and the New Testament writings for legend to displace historical truth.[16]

In fact, I later learned that a creed of the early church—affirming that Jesus died for our sins, was resurrected, and appeared to many witnesses—has been traced back to within three to eight years after Jesus' death. This statement of faith, reported by the apostle Paul in First Corinthians 15:3–7, is based on firsthand accounts and is a very early confirmation of the core of the Gospel.[17]

Piece by piece, my mental jigsaw puzzle was coming together.

THE POWER OF PROPHECY

Next I turned to the Bible's prophecies, an area I was especially cynical about. I had written a lot of articles over the years on predictions about the future—it was one of those New Year's stories that all beginning reporters got stuck doing—and I knew how few prognostications actually came true. For instance, every year people in Chicago insist that the Cubs are going to clinch the World Series, and *that* certainly hasn't come true in my lifetime!

Even so, the more I analyzed the Old Testament prophecies, the more convinced I became that they constitute amazing historical evidence to support the claims that Jesus is the Messiah and Son of God.

For example, I read Isaiah 53 in the Old Testament and found it to be an absolutely uncanny description of Jesus' being crucified—and yet it was written more than 700 years before the fact. That's like my trying to predict how the Cubs will do in the year 2693! In all, there are about five dozen major prophecies concerning the Messiah, and the more I studied them, the more difficulty I had in trying to explain them away.

My first line of defense was that Jesus may have intentionally maneuvered His life to fulfill the prophecies so that He would be mistaken for the long-awaited Messiah. For instance, Zechariah 9:9 foretold that the Messiah would ride a donkey into Jerusalem. Maybe when Jesus was getting ready to enter the town, He told His disciples, "Go fetch Me a donkey. I want to fool these people into thinking I'm the Messiah because I'm really anxious to be tortured to death!"

But that argument fell apart when I read prophecies about events that Jesus never could have arranged, such as the place of His birth, which the prophet Micah foretold seven hundred years in advance, and His ancestry, how He was born, how He was betrayed for a specific amount of money, how He was put to death, how His bones remained unbroken (unlike the two criminals who were crucified with Him), how the soldiers cast lots for His clothing, and on and on.[18]

My second line of defense was that Jesus wasn't the only person to whom these prophecies pointed. Maybe several people in history have fit these predictions, but Jesus happened to have a better public relations agent and so now He's the one everyone remembers.

But reading a book by Peter Stoner, professor emeritus of science at Westmont College, dismantled that objection. Stoner worked with six hundred students to calculate the mathematical probability of just eight of the Old Testament prophecies being fulfilled in any one person living down to the present time.[19] The probability was one chance in ten to the seventeenth power. That's a figure with seventeen zeroes behind it!

To try to comprehend that enormous number, I did some calculations. I imagined the entire world being covered with white tile that was one-and-a-half inches square—every bit of dry land on the planet—with the bottom of just one tile painted red.

Then I pictured a person being allowed to wander for a lifetime around all seven continents. He would be permitted to bend down only one time and pick up a single piece of tile. What are the odds it would be the one tile whose reverse side was painted red? The odds would be the same as just eight of the Old Testament prophecies coming true in any one person throughout history!

That was impressive enough, but then Stoner analyzed forty-eight prophecies. His conclusion was that there would be one chance in ten to the 157th power that they would come true in any one person in history.[20] That's a number with 157 zeroes behind it!

I did some research and learned that atoms are so small that it takes a million of them lined up to equal the width of a human hair. I also interviewed scientists about their estimate of the number of atoms in the entire known universe.

And while that's an incredibly large number, I concluded that the odds of forty-eight Old Testament prophecies' coming true in any one individual are the same as a person randomly finding a single predetermined atom among all the atoms in a *trillion trillion trillion trillion billion* universes the size of our universe!

Jesus said He came to fulfill the prophecies. He said, "Everything must be fulfilled that is written about me in the Law of Moses, the Prophets and the Psalms."[21] I was beginning to believe that they were fulfilled—only in Jesus Christ.

I asked myself if someone offered me a business deal with

just one chance in ten to the 157th power that I'd lose, how much would I invest? I'd put everything I owned into a sure-fire winner like that! And I was starting to think, "With those kind of odds, maybe I should think about investing my life in Christ."

THE REALITY OF THE RESURRECTION

Since it's central to Christianity, I also spent quite a bit of time analyzing the historical evidence for the resurrection of Jesus. I certainly wasn't the first skeptic to do that. Many have gone through the same exercise and emerged as Christians.

For instance, a British journalist and lawyer named Frank Morison set out to write the authoritative book exposing the resurrection as a myth. However, after painstakingly studying the evidence, he became a Christian, saying there was no question that the resurrection has "a deep and profoundly historical basis."[22] The book he eventually wrote about his spiritual investigation gave me an attorney's incisive analysis of the resurrection accounts.

Another legal perspective came from Simon Greenleaf, the brilliant professor of evidence who is credited with helping Harvard Law School first achieve its reputation for excellence. Greenleaf authored one of the finest American treatises ever written on the topic of what constitutes legal evidence.

In fact, even the U.S. Supreme Court quoted it. The *London Law Journal* once said that Greenleaf knew more about the laws of evidence than "all the lawyers who adorn the courts of Europe."[23]

Greenleaf scoffed at the resurrection until a student challenged him to check it out for himself. He methodically applied the legal tests of evidence and became convinced that the resurrection was an actual historical event. The Jewish professor then committed his life to Christ.[24]

In summary, the evidence for the resurrection is that Jesus was killed by crucifixion and was stabbed by a spear; He was pronounced dead by experts; He was wrapped in bandages containing seventy-five pounds of spices; He was placed in a tomb; a huge rock was rolled in front of the entrance (according to one ancient account, so big that twenty men couldn't move it); and the tomb was guarded by highly disciplined soldiers.

Yet, three days later the tomb was discovered empty, and eyewitnesses proclaimed to their death that Jesus had appeared to them.

Who had a motive to steal the body? The disciples weren't about to conceal it so they could be tortured to death for lying about it. The Jewish and Roman leaders would have loved to have paraded the body up and down Main Street in Jerusalem; certainly that would have instantly killed this budding religion that they had spent so much time trying to squelch.

But what happened is that over a period of forty days, Jesus appeared alive twelve different times to more than 515 people— to skeptics like Thomas and James, and sometimes to groups, sometimes to individuals, sometimes indoors, sometimes outdoors in broad daylight. He talked with people and even ate with them.

Several years later, when the apostle Paul mentioned that there had been eyewitnesses to the resurrection, he noted that many of them were still alive, as if to say to first-century doubters, "Go confirm it with them if you don't believe me."[25]

In fact, if you were to call to the witness stand every person who actually saw the resurrected Jesus, and if you were to cross-examine each one of them for only fifteen minutes, and if you did this around the clock without any breaks, you would be listening to firsthand testimony for more than five solid days.

Compared to the trials I had covered, this was an avalanche of evidence. More puzzle pieces locked into place.

DIGGING FOR THE TRUTH

I looked at archaeology and discovered that it has confirmed the biblical record time after time. Admittedly, there are some issues still to be resolved. However, one eminent archaeologist, Dr. Nelson Gleuck, said: "It may be stated categorically that no archaeological discovery has ever controverted a biblical reference. Scores of archaeological findings have been made that confirm in clear outline or in exact detail historical statements in the Bible."[26]

I was especially fascinated by the story of Sir William Ramsay of Oxford University in England, one of history's greatest archaeologists. He was an atheist; in fact, he was the son of atheists. He spent twenty-five years doing archaeological digs to try to disprove the book of Acts, which was written by the historian Luke who also penned the Gospel bearing his name.

But instead of discrediting Luke's account, Ramsay's discoveries kept supporting it. Finally, he concluded that Luke was one of the most accurate historians who ever lived. Bolstered by the archaeological evidence, Ramsay became a Christian.[27]

Then I said, "Okay, so there's evidence that the New Testament is historically reliable. But what evidence is there for Jesus *outside* the Bible?"

I was amazed to find out that there are about a dozen non-Christian writers from ancient history who cite historic details about the life of Jesus, including the fact that He did amazing things, that He was known as a virtuous person, that He was called the Messiah, that He was crucified, that the sky went dark while He hung on the cross, that His disciples said He had returned from the dead, and that they worshiped Him as God.[28]

Actually, this is just a brief overview of my spiritual investigation, since I delved into a lot more details than can be described here. And I don't want to suggest this was merely an antiseptic, academic exercise. There was plenty of emotion involved, as Chapter 9 will describe. But it seemed as if everywhere I turned was more confirmation of the reliability of the biblical account of the life, death, and resurrection of Jesus Christ.

SOLVING THE PUZZLE

I sorted through the evidence for a year and nine months, until Sunday, November 8, 1981, after I had returned home from church. I was alone in my bedroom, and I concluded that the time had arrived to reach a verdict.

Christianity had not been absolutely proven. If it had, there would be no room for faith. But when I weighed the facts, I concluded that the historical evidence clearly supports the claims of Christ beyond any reasonable doubt. In fact, based on what I had learned, it would have taken more faith to remain an atheist than to become a Christian!

So, after I had put the last piece of my mental jigsaw puzzle into place, I figuratively stepped back to see the picture I had been systematically piecing together in my mind for almost two years.

It was a portrait of Jesus Christ, the Son of God.

Like the former skeptic Thomas, I responded by declaring: "My Lord and my God!"

Afterward, I walked into the kitchen, where Leslie was standing next to Alison in front of the sink. Our daughter was five years old at the time, and by standing on her toes and stretching, she was barely able to reach the kitchen faucet for the first time.

"Look, Daddy, look!" she exclaimed. "I can touch it! I can touch it!"

"Honey, that's great," I told her as I gave her a hug. Then I said to Leslie, "You know, that's exactly how I feel. I've been reaching for someone for a long time, and today I was finally able to touch Him."

She knew what I was saying. With tears in our eyes, we embraced.

As it turned out, Leslie and her friends had been praying for me almost daily throughout my spiritual journey. Often,

Leslie's prayers had focused on this verse from the Old Testament:

I will give you a new heart and put a new spirit in you; I will remove from you your heart of stone and give you a heart of flesh.[29]

Thank God, He has been faithful to that promise.

TAKE-AWAY POINTS

That's the story of one Unchurched Harry's spiritual journey. Of course, there's no "typical" path to Christ. Some people are prompted to seek God because of a crisis in their lives; others because of an aching emptiness. But here are eight broad principles distilled from my story that might help you in reaching the Unchurched Harrys and Marys in your life:

• Evangelism is most often a process, not a sudden event. Generally, the Holy Spirit works over time in a person's life. While conversion happens at a specific moment, there is usually much that precedes it. Yet many Christians and churches are only geared to treat evangelism as an event—a decision that needs to be made *right now*, rather than a choice that frequently comes after a period of discovery. Actually, prematurely pressing for a commitment can be counter-productive.

• As Leslie demonstrated, many times unchurched people are willing to visit a church if they're invited by a friend who has already opened up spiritual issues through personal conversations. But there is a potential downside to this that I'll discuss at the end of chapter 5.

• Women can have a significant influence with men on religious issues, as Leslie did with me. This was quantified in a 1992 study that examined the role of wives and girlfriends in reaching British men with the Gospel. "Perhaps it's only with their wives or girlfriends that the barriers are down far enough for men to discuss these very personal matters," said researcher Pam Hanley.[30]

• In trying to reach a friend with the Gospel, even mature

Christians often need to partner with a church that offers services or periodic events that are sensitive to seekers.

• "Apologetics," or using evidence and reasoning to defend the faith, is critically important in penetrating the skepticism of many secular people today. This is especially true for non-believers who are in professions that deal with facts and figures, such as engineering, science, journalism, medicine, and law.

• Many irreligious people avoid church because of negative church experiences they had as a child. However, these biases can be overcome if a church thinks through the way that it will be perceived by unchurched visitors and then shapes its ministry accordingly, without altering the Gospel.

• Once a person sincerely begins to check out Christianity, it's only a matter of time before he'll discover the truth about God. The Bible says, "You will seek me and find me when you seek me with all your heart."[31] However, it's important to realize that the seeking process itself is a response to the Holy Spirit's work. It is He who was sent to "convict the world of guilt in regard to sin and righteousness and judgment" because we matter so much to God.[32] Apart from that, none of us would seek God at all.[33]

• As Leslie found, there's no substitute for asking God to intervene in a person's life. James said that the prayer of a righteous person is powerful and effective.[34]

Now let's look at some specific attitudes that may be influencing your unchurched friends to steer clear of God and the church—and some ways that you can respond.

4
UNDERSTANDING YOUR UNCHURCHED FRIENDS, PART I

Smile, Harry and Mary! They're taking your picture!

In the last few years, researchers have been working hard to come up with a composite portrait of the average unchurched American. As never before, their demographic analysis has helped bring into focus the 55 to 78 million unchurched adults who live in the U.S. For instance, surveys show that the unchurched:

- Are more commonly male than female;
- Frequently are either single or married to a person of another religious background;
- Are likely to live in a western state;
- Have a median age of 35, two years younger than the average American.
- Have an income of $32,800 a year ($4,200 more than the typical American).

• Are more educated than the norm, with 32% composed of college graduates.

• Almost always have some church experience in their background, a slight majority being Protestant.[1]

While these statistics give us a snapshot of what Unchurched Harry and Mary look like, what's really important is what's inside their heads. Before we begin to strategize how we as individuals and churches can effectively bring them the Gospel, we need to climb into their minds and delve into their attitudes and motivations.

Of course, their mindset can vary significantly according to several factors. Opinions about God and church differ between baby boomers (those born between 1946 and 1964) and baby busters (born between 1965 and 1983); females and males; Southerners and Westerners; and among blacks, whites, and Hispanics.

Based on my own experience as a non-Christian; my interaction with unchurched people; input from pastors, psychologists, and others who have dealt with them; and in-depth surveys by pollsters George Gallup, Jr., George Barna, and others, I've reached some general conclusions that might be helpful in understanding them.

So here are some observations about the unchurched. For convenience and consistency, I'll generally use Harry's name, but as I said earlier, most of the comments apply equally to Unchurched Mary. As you read, consider whether there are implications for the way you personally befriend unchurched individuals and how your church is geared to reach them.

Observation #1: Harry has rejected church, but that doesn't necessarily mean he has rejected God.

This is a crucial distinction. Unchurched Harry often is a "religious" person—in fact, he could be intensely interested in spiritual matters—but he may be turned off to the church because he sees it as an archaic and irrelevant institution. This means that he may be more open to talking about God and considering the claims of Christ than people think.

Actually, only about 13% of Americans are atheists or agnostics.[2] However, while most people say that they believe in God, the real question is, "Which species of deity are they talking about?" As one researcher commented, "Americans seem to use God to refer to a general principle of good in life—or, sometimes, he (or she) is the creator who set off the Big Bang but doesn't intervene in human affairs."[3]

Even so, many unchurched people exhibit a desire to interact with their Creator. In 1992, *Newsweek* magazine featured a cover story called "Talking to God" in which it observed with some astonishment, "This week, if you believe at all in opinion surveys, more of us will pray than will go to work, or exercise, or have sexual relations."[4]

The article cited new research saying that 91% of American women and 85% of men pray—but perhaps most amazing was the finding that one out of five atheists and agnostics prays each day![5] The article didn't specify who the recipient of those prayers was supposed to be.

Many unchurched people consider themselves to be Christians. In fact, a majority of the unchurched—52%—claim they have made a personal commitment to Jesus Christ that is important in their life.[6]

Yet they don't feel compelled to attend church. Unchurched people are virtually unanimous in believing that they can be a good Christian independent from any religious institution, apparently subscribing to the cliché, "I can worship God better while walking in the woods than I can inside a building."[7] Amazingly, two-thirds of *churched* people agree with that,[8] despite the biblical admonition: "Let us not give up meeting together, as some are in the habit of doing."[9]

So for many unchurched people, their motto seems to be, "I believe in God; I just don't believe in church." Or as John

Stott sums up their attitude: "Hostile to the church, friendly to Jesus Christ."[10]

Many of them think that church is unnecessary, irrelevant, and unable to help them find meaning in life. Unfortunately, they're speaking from personal experience, since research shows that most unchurched people used to attend church regularly.

"Thus, most unchurched adults have made a *conscious decision* not to attend church," Barna concludes. "It is the rare adult who avoids the local church out of lack of experience with such religious behavior."[11]

The reasons for Unchurched Harry's defection from church vary, but an overwhelming 91% of non-Christians believe that the church isn't very sensitive to their needs.[12] And in the eyes of our self-centered, consumer-oriented society, that's the ultimate sin.

So getting Harry back inside means that the church is going to have to overcome the objections that drove him away in the first place, without compromising the Gospel. That's what much of this book is about.

It's encouraging, though, that there's a vast reservoir of religious interest in this country. My wife, Leslie, was reminded of that when she began inviting neighborhood women to a Bible study in our home a few years ago. She expected to receive a cold shoulder from some, but to her surprise, everybody wanted to come. All of them expressed curiosity in learning more about the Bible.

As *Newsweek* concluded, "In allegedly rootless, materialistic, self-centered America, there is also a hunger for a personal experience of God."[13]

Observation #2: Harry is morally adrift, but he secretly wants an anchor.

I know what it's like to live a life of moral relativism, where every day I made fresh ethical choices based on self-interest and expediency. Writing my own rules freed me up to satisfy my desires without anybody looking over my shoulder. Frankly, it's an exhilarating way to live—for a while.

Certainly America has been living that way for quite some time. That's what James Patterson and Peter Kim concluded after conducting a national study in which they asked people to be brutally honest about how they *really* live.

The first chapter of their eye-opening book, *The Day America Told The Truth*, says: "In the 1950s and even in the early 1960s, there was something much closer to a moral consensus in America . . . . There is absolutely no moral consensus at all in the 1990s. Everyone is making up their own personal moral codes— their own Ten Commandments."[14]

Remember the original Ten Commandments, the ones Moses received from God? Well, only 13% of Americans say they still believe in all of them.[15]

Instead, these are some of today's commandments, including the percentage of Americans who follow them: I will steal from those who won't really miss it (74%); I will lie when it suits me (64%); I will waste the equivalent of a full day of work each week (50%); I will cheat on my spouse (53%); I will lie on my tax returns (30%); and I am willing to put my lover at risk of disease (31%).[16]

What a scathing indictment! Proliferation of situational ethics in recent years has plunged the country into a moral quagmire. Sixty-nine percent of Americans adhere to the attitude that there's no absolute moral standard, but that ethics should fluctuate according to the situation.[17] And, of course, what causes that fluctuation is usually our own selfish agenda.

That's how many Harrys live. Yet numbers of them are beginning to conclude that moral anarchy isn't all that Hugh Hefner once painted it to be.

After all, it takes emotional energy to make day-to-day ethical choices with no baseline to start with and to keep track of a tangle of conflicting decisions. Often, there's a free-floating sense of guilt, and inevitably there's harm caused to oneself and others. Although I would have denied it back then, I think I would have welcomed someone drawing reasonable boundaries for me to live within. There's evidence that others feel this way, too. If you look at the churches that are most successful in attracting irreligious people, you'll find that they generally aren't the liberal ones with lenient attitudes but are those that cling to the Bible's clear-cut moral stands. One interesting study found that many baby boomers "are not turned off by religion, just indifferent to churches that do not stand out from the surrounding culture."[18]

Gary Collins and Timothy Clinton studied baby boomers and concluded that millions of them "feel like they are drifting, with no absolute values or beliefs to which they can anchor their lives. Many feel empty inside, without firm standards of right and wrong, and with no valid guidelines for raising children, maintaining a marriage, building careers, doing business, or finding God. Now, perhaps more than at any time in baby-boomer history, these core-less people are looking for truth, identity, and something to believe in that will give their lives a real center."[19]

With many Unchurched Harrys secretly seeking moral direction for their lives, the door is cracked open for Christians to share the Bible's guidelines for living. It's important that we think through how that plan is articulated, as this next point will explain.

Observation #3: Harry resists rules but responds to reasons.

Unchurched Harry doesn't like to be told what to do. He recoils when people tell him that he ought to live a certain way because the Bible says he should. After all, he's not convinced yet that the Bible really is God's revelation. Besides, there has been a society-wide erosion of respect for authority, and Harry thinks he's better qualified than anyone to decide what rules he should abide by.

Yet, at the same time, Harry is generally open to reasoning. When we as Christians lay out for him the underlying thinking behind the moral boundaries that God has drawn for us, and when he understands the benefits of abiding by God's commands, he's much more receptive to following them.

For example, I met recently with a businessman who confided in me that he was living with his girlfriend. Now, there certainly isn't any shortage of Bible verses I could have read to him to point out that he had strayed from God's laws. What proved more effective was for me to explain to him the emotional, psychological, physical, and relational damage that can result from having intimate relations without the security of a marriage.

After painting the downside of his behavior, I then cited Scripture against nonmarital sex and said, "Don't you see—God said that unmarried sexual relations are out of bounds not to frustrate you, or to arbitrarily spoil your fun, but because He loves you so much that He wants to spare you these negative consequences."

Then I painted the benefits of living God's way—and Unchurched Harry is always ready to listen when the topic is how he can benefit.

So, for the most part, Unchurched Harry doesn't respond well to someone who predicates a command on, "Thus sayeth the Lord." He wants to see the wisdom behind changing his ways, which opens up terrific opportunities for Christians to explain how God's guidelines for our lives are reasonable, practical, and just, and how they are motivated by His great concern for us.

Keeping this in our own minds is important, too. At times we can be so offended by Harry's immoral lifestyle that we can become judgmental and condemning, saying to ourselves, "I hope he gets what he deserves." That sets up an unhealthy we-versus-them mentality.

But when we remind ourselves that God wants Harry to bring his lifestyle into compliance with his moral laws because

He deeply loves Harry and wants to protect him from harm, it softens our own attitude toward Harry. And, believe me, Harry can sense the difference as we interact with him.

Observation #4: Harry doesn't understand Christianity, but he's also ignorant about what he claims to believe in.

Sometimes we fall prey to the misconception that Unchurched Harry has already analyzed the Christian faith, seriously considered its tenets, and come to the reasoned conclusion that it's simply not true.

We think his lifestyle is a deliberate choice he has made after thoughtfully weighing and rejecting the Christian option. As a result, when we begin talking to him, we make the false assumption that he is further along in processing Christianity than he really is.

The truth is that, in many instances, Harry is a Christianity illiterate. Although he probably owns a Bible, the chances are he has never made an honest effort to read and understand it. He doesn't know Moses from Paul, or Abraham from Peter. He's full of misinformation, such as that the Bible says the earth is 10,000 years old, or that Scripture is chock-full of contradictions.

Most Americans can't even name the four gospels; six out of ten don't know who delivered the Sermon on the Mount.[20] When non-Christians were asked if they knew why Christians celebrate Easter, 46% couldn't give an accurate answer.[21]

Their view of Christian theology is often garbled and inaccurate, perhaps a hodge-podge of New Age thinking grafted onto old Sunday school lessons. It's incredible the theological concoctions people can conjure up!

When I talk to unchurched people, I'm frequently amazed at the elementary nature of the issues they raise. I'm all geared up to argue ten reasons why the accounts of Christ's resurrection are historically reliable, and they're asking, "Who was this Jesus anyway?"

The key is, *assume nothing*. When talking to Unchurched

Harry, always let him give you his version of what Christianity is all about. Take the time to gauge his level of knowledge. Listen for misinformation. Ask him to define the words he uses, since "sin" and "grace" may have totally different meanings to him than to you. After gently probing his base of knowledge, you'll be better equipped to begin talking to him about Christ at an appropriate level. You may even find he already agrees with some basic Christian doctrines that you had been planning to try to convince him are true.

But it's important to understand something else about Harry: In many instances he doesn't even have a handle on what he does believe. One study showed that 51% of Americans have no philosophy of life![22]

Lots of times I've found that Harry has never really thought through his own belief system well enough to be able to articulate or defend it. Sometimes it seems that he's making up his beliefs as he tells them to me. Listen to this 24-year-old Denver resident talk about his life philosophy:

> You know, once in a psychology class I was asked what the meaning of life is. It was for an exam that should have taken four hours, and I finished it in fifteen minutes. (Laughs.) The professor had phrased the question, "What is life?" Well, I just sat around, kinda looked around for a little bit, and I rephrased it to say, "Life is everything." Turned it in and got an A on it. You think about it, you know, people talkin' about the chemical composition of a table or a tree . . . life is everything. Everything that we know is life.
>
> For me, there's a oneness, I guess, with nature (I don't wanna sound like a granola-head when I'm sayin' this), but it's getting back to nature. There's a feeling that I get when I ski that, you know, I'm one with whoever created that particular mountain at that given time. [23]

Not exactly a well-developed, fully integrated philosophy of life. Yet, often that's the sort of answer I get—in varying degrees of sophistication—when I ask Harry about his beliefs.

In fact, one of the most effective evangelistic approaches I've learned is to ask Harry to describe what he believes about God, and then let him talk. And talk. And talk. I listen with interest, I request details, I urge him to go deeper, and I ask him to define the words he's using.

You see, sometimes he has never verbalized with any depth what he believes, and as he describes his views of God and life, they begin to sound flimsy and cliché-ridden even to him. He may realize for the first time that he doesn't know as much as he thought.

Then I ask him what his truth source is. In other words, where did he get this viewpoint? Sometimes it was a friend who told him about reincarnation. Or he saw a TV show about meditation techniques. Or he read a book by Shirley McLain, or an article on Islam.

Next I ask him to assess the accuracy of that truth source. If he's going to pin his eternity on this source of information about God, then he ought to make sure it's reliable. Often, just asking the right questions can help Harry recognize that his personal theology rests on a feeble foundation.

Finally, I help him see the firm foundation on which Christianity is based. We have a truth source that's historically defensible, archaeologically sound, based on eyewitness accounts, substantiated by outside writings, and whose supernatural nature has been established by fulfilled prophecies and the millions of lives it has transformed.

Harry is usually much more receptive to talking about the basis for Christianity after he has come to the realization that his own personal beliefs aren't as well-developed or well-supported as he liked to pretend.

Observation #5: Harry has legitimate questions about spiritual matters, but he doesn't expect answers from Christians.

He was Jewish, a comedian by profession, and he cornered me after I had participated in a panel discussion about the credibility of Christianity. In a somewhat accusatory and belligerent tone, he began pummeling me with challenges about the resurrection of Christ.

As we went back and forth with questions, answers, and adamant statements, our encounter grew more heated. Our voices got louder and a crowd gathered around. In fact, an off-duty FBI agent tried to break us up because he thought we would get into a fight.

Half an hour later, the comedian stuck out his hand in a gesture of friendship. "Thanks for being willing to argue with me," he said. "I really appreciate that you stood up for what you believe."

"What do you mean?" I asked.

"I've been to a bunch of priests and pastors and ministers, and when I'd raise an argument against the resurrection, they'd just smile and say, 'Well, *touché*! That's a good point,' and they'd walk away. They wouldn't defend what they believe, and it made me mad. If they were going to teach it, why wouldn't they defend it? I started to wonder whether anybody believed in this Christianity stuff enough to debate it."

I apologized for having gotten emotional during our discussion, but he said, "No, that's what I needed. I *needed* to argue about this." And now, he said, he would be willing to more calmly look for answers.

Unchurched Harry has a whole range of questions about Christianity, and they deserve answers. Whatever the nature of his inquiry, even if it sounds frivolous or elementary, it should be considered valid if it's hanging him up on his spiritual journey.

But, unfortunately, many Harrys look at churches and

imagine a sign out front that says, *No questions allowed*. As the pastor at a fundamentalist church in Texas shouted just before an altar call: "You don't have a question to ask; you've got a decision to make!"

The church should be a place where questions are welcomed, even encouraged. When Unchurched Harry senses that his objections will be respected and given reasoned responses, he's much more willing to give church a try.

Ed Dobson has demonstrated that in Grand Rapids, Michigan, where his church decided to keep its traditional Sunday services but to add a seeker service on Saturday nights. From the beginning, one important feature of those services has been that Ed, wearing casual clothes and sitting on a stool, would respond to any written question from those in attendance. The inquiries range from "I'm gay. Is that okay?" to "Does God punish us with trials and tribulations?"

Each week his outreach service at Calvary Church, promoted on billboards around town, attracts hundreds of people who would shun "regular church." This kind of outreach is effective because Unchurched Harry imagines a sign outside that says, *Your Questions Are Welcomed*.

Similarly, when you're interacting with Unchurched Harry on an individual level, the manner in which you respond to his questions is extremely important. Many times, the first question he raises is a sort of "trial balloon." He wants to see whether you'll laugh at him, belittle him for his ignorance, dismiss his inquiry as trivial, or take the question seriously.

So his initial questions aren't the top ones on his mind but are just the ones he feels safest in expressing. If you validate his right to raise issues and you respond with sincerity, he'll be more willing to go deeper and ask about the issues that are really stymieing his spiritual journey.

There have been times when I've been talking to Unchurched Harry and he's prefaced a question with, "Now, don't laugh at this next one." That's his way of saying, *I'm going to get vulnerable here and ask something that could make me sound stupid. So cut me some slack.* Unless you make him feel comfortable, he'll never get to the questions that are truly hanging him up.

One way I legitimize the inquiry process is to assure Harry at the outset, "You know, you're doing exactly what God wants you to do. He honors those who honestly check Him out. The Bible says in Hebrews 11:6 that God 'rewards those who earnestly seek Him.' So you should have confidence; you're doing the right thing by asking whatever questions you have on your mind."

Observation #6: Harry doesn't just ask, "Is Christianity true?" Often, he's asking: "Does Christianity work?"

I was talking with a Christian leader from a large midwestern university, and he was telling me about how students have changed in the last few decades. "Kids these days aren't asking, 'What's true?' " he said. "That's what college kids asked in the '60s. Today, kids are asking, 'What can help me deal with my pain?' It seems as though every kid I disciple comes from a dysfunctional family, and he's trying to process his pain."

The nature of Harry's questions is evolving over time. For many, especially the younger generation, truth isn't an issue because they have become convinced that all religious viewpoints are equally valid. It's the old, "You have your truth and I have mine."

We need to help Harry understand the absolute and unchanging truth of Christ, but we should also explain how Christ is available to help him in practical ways to heal his hurts and help him deal with everyday living. We need to communicate that Christianity isn't just for the tomorrow of his eternity but also for the today of his life.

I've discussed this at length with Martin Robinson, an astute observer of the British religious scene. He recently made this observation about Britain, although it's certainly germane to the U.S.:

At one time the most important question in our society was, "Is this true?" That is the question that most Christian apologetics are designed to answer. "Is it true that Jesus rose from the dead?" "Is the Bible accurate?" and so on. However, the impact of secularism is such that many no longer ask that question in the field of morals and faith.

It is assumed that since all faith and morality are firmly in the area of opinion and that all opinions are equally valid, the only thing that really matters is whether or not they work: "Does it work?" is the question that arises again and again. Never mind if the suggested formula is derived from Hinduism, Buddhism, the occult, or Christianity—the main question asked is, "Does it work?"[24]

Gary Collins and Timothy Clinton made a similar comment concerning baby busters, the generation that follows the baby boomers in the U.S.:

They learned to expect that their needs should be met, jobs would be provided, money would be available, and problems would be solved. The result is a generation of young adults who want and expect everything right away. Life is to be lived for the present.

There is little awareness of a philosophy that says we should make long-range plans, or work hard today so things will be better tomorrow. This is a "now" generation that has little interest in any religion that talks about sacrifices, heaven, or "the sweet by-and-by." They want to hear about a faith that works now and brings immediate results.[25]

Our challenge, then, is to help this new generation of Unchurched Harrys understand that Christianity *does* work, that is, that the God of the Bible offers us supernatural wisdom and assistance in our struggles, difficulties, and recovery from past hurts.

But we need to communicate that the *reason* it works is

because it's *true*. Because Christ, at a point in history, had the power to overcome the grave, we can have access to that same kind of supernatural power to cope with the difficulties that face us day to day. And because the Bible is God's revelation to His people, it contains a kind of practical and effective help that's unmatched by mere human philosophers.

In other words, there's a cause and effect—the "cause" is that Christianity is *true*, and there's solid historical evidence to support that; the "effect" or result is that Christianity *works*, and there are millions of Christians who would attest to that.

Some people get mixed up in this area. They believe that because something appears to work, it must therefore be based on truth. For example, one prominent nature worshiper in Northern California says that she doesn't want to hit a deer while driving at night, so:

> As she sets out in her car, Anne imagines a blue light circling her vehicle clockwise three times, then silently chants, "Three times around, three times about/A world within, a world without." Then she adds a silent prayer to Artemis, goddess of the hunt, "to protect the deer and tell them I'm coming. I imagine this as a psychic warning system." Anne believes wholeheartedly in this practice. "It works!" she says. "I have a friend who's hit twelve deer in five years. I've never hit one."[26]

Can you see how muddled thinking can lead to false conclusions? To deduce on the basis of a few missed deer that a belief system is valid turns logic on its head. As far as Christianity is concerned, we're not saying it's true *because* it works; we're saying Christianity is true *and therefore* it works.[27]

So Christians need to continue to marshal the historic, archaeological, prophetic, and other evidence that Jesus is the one and only Son of God. But we shouldn't stop there. We should be ready to go the next step and tell Harry that because that's true, there are meaningful implications for his life today—

for his marriage, his friendships, his career, his recovery from past pain, and so on.

Observation #7: Harry doesn't just want to know something; he wants to experience it.

As a young teenager, Rex began asking, "Is there or is there not a God? And what's the bottom line, game plan, or purpose of life?" He read books and talked to friends and adults in search of answers yet remained unsatisfied. After his intellectual exploration failed, he sought the truth through experiences.

For him, that meant 100 to 150 LSD trips, starting in 1966 when he was fifteen years old. "And I would say that those experiences have had a profound influence in terms of my view of the world," he said.

Today, Rex is an atheist, and he says he makes his moral decisions "solely on the basis of the pleasure principle."[28]

For many Unchurched Harrys who are on a spiritual journey, experience—not evidence—is their mode of discovery. For Rex, they were drug experiences, and they ushered him into dark territory. However, many others are on a constructive and positive search for a personal experience with God.

"We want, as a generation, to move beyond philosophical discussions of religions to the actual experience of God in our lives," said baby-boomer expert Doug Murren. "The boomer heart, like every human heart, has always cried out for a personal experience with God."[29]

In fact, one out of four unchurched people say they already have had a "particularly powerful religious insight or awakening."[30]

The objective of evangelism should be to bring Unchurched Harry into a personal encounter *with* God, not just to merely pass on information *about* God. Harry wants to actually meet this Jesus Christ we're talking about; he wants to sense the comfort and power of the Holy Spirit.

Murren decries the sterility of many church services in

which there's no sense of God's presence and attributes the growth of pentecostal and charismatic fellowships largely to the fact that "their theology is friendly toward spiritual experiences."[31]

I look at it this way: *If* Christianity is true, *if* Jesus is real, and *if* he did sacrifice Himself for our sins, then what would you expect church services to be like? You wouldn't expect them to be stilted, stale, and stiff; you would expect them to be sincere, stimulating, and spirited!

If Christ is alive, His church shouldn't be dead. We should be able to go there with the expectation of actually engaging with God.

So if we keep our church services tuned to God, prayerfully encourage the Holy Spirit to be active, and endeavor to connect with God in creative ways, we're more likely to create a climate conducive to Harry's quest for a personal experience with Him.

Observation #8: Harry doesn't want to be somebody's project, but he would like to be somebody's friend.

Have you ever had a "friendship" with strings attached? In other words, you felt the person would be your buddy only if you'd continue to do him favors, play golf with him once a week, or give him free professional advice. These relationships are inherently insecure, and over a period of time, resentment inevitably boils to the surface.

That's how Unchurched Harry feels when our behavior suggests that the main reason we're his friend is because we want to convert him. Maybe we don't call him as often after he rebuffed our invitation to come to a men's breakfast at church. Or maybe he hears that when we get together with our Christian friends to talk about our evangelistic efforts, we disclose private details of his personal life.

After a while, Harry feels like a case study. After all, he says, if this were a *real* friendship—based on affinity, mutual interest, concern for each other, and keeping confidences—it wouldn't be dependent on whether we succeed in bringing him to Christ.

This can be a downside to relational evangelism unless the Christian determines from the outset that his friendship with Harry is going to be authentic and unconditional. That is, the Christian's attitude should be to genuinely care about Harry as a friend regardless of his spiritual progress.

You see, Harry is hungering for close friendships. He desperately wants a confidant who cares about him. In fact, there's a difference between Unchurched Harry and Mary: *It's Harry who's more desperate for meaningful relationships and less equipped to find them.*

"Women make friends more easily than men do," said David W. Smith in his book *Men Without Friends.* "They form and sustain relationships at a more qualitative level than do men."[32] Social science researcher Daniel Levinson puts it bluntly: "Close friendship with a man or a woman is rarely experienced by American men."[33]

Smith describes several factors that hinder men from making and maintaining relationships with other men, including the fact that as youngsters most were encouraged to suppress their emotions, to be competitive, to keep their personal needs and longings deep inside, and to look up to role models who are independent and impersonal.[34]

Compounding these difficulties is that we don't stick around long enough in our fast-paced culture to put down deep relational roots. The average American moves fourteen times in his lifetime and every decade about half the average town's population moves.[35]

As a result, men have a craving for community with others. So two of the most persuasive evangelistic steps we can take are to:

• Demonstrate the unconditional love of Christ in our relationship with Harry;

• Let him know about the kind of rich, deep relationships that can exist when two men have God in common.

The Bible has numerous examples of close friendships between men. Jesus did ministry in community with twelve men and had an even closer relationship with John, Peter, and James. David and Jonathan were "one in spirit."[36] Paul was so close to Timothy that he called him "my true son."[37] The Bible defines a real friend as a person who "sticks closer than a brother."[38]

Someone once said that the depth of a friendship is determined by the depth of what you hold in common. If your common bond is an interest in tennis, chances are you'll have a shallow relationship. What I've found in my own life is that when the common bond is Jesus Christ, there's a potential for a deep, abiding friendship in which you're knit together at the soul.

Unfortunately, as Smith observed, the modern church is often "a place where Christians live alone together."[39] Instead of being places of true community, too often they're places of conflict or superficiality, violating the biblical mandate for Christians to "carry each other's burdens" and thereby "fulfill the law of Christ."[40]

This is important: *We run the risk of repelling Unchurched Harry unless he sees in our churches the kind of authentic community, honest accountability, freely offered forgiveness, and mutual care that Scripture calls for.* That's a challenge that must be addressed, modeled, and taught from the top leadership of every church.

After all, those elements are fundamental to what it means to be a Christian. Church leaders would do well to consider Gary Inrig's analogy in which he likens the Christian life to a crossword puzzle:

"Until both the vertical and horizontal lines are finished, it is incomplete. To know the Lord Jesus involves not only a vertical dimension with the living God but also horizontal relationships within the family of God. A beautiful symmetry results. By abiding in Christ, I am able to love my fellow believers. By loving them, I abide more deeply in the Father's love. By abiding more deeply, I love more deeply, and on and on it moves."[41]

On a practical level, introducing small groups into a church can create great opportunities for Christians to go deep with each other. As Harry sees his Christian friends benefiting from being in community with others, he'll be drawn toward the church.

You see, Harry's attitude softens considerably when he sees the church not as an institution but as a caring community where his relational longings can be fulfilled.

Yet the flip side of that is true, too. As we'll see in the next chapter, where I'll offer some additional observations, Harry's opinion about the church plummets when he merely sees it as another imposing and impersonal institution of society.

5
UNDERSTANDING
YOUR UNCHURCHED
FRIENDS, PART II

Americans are fed up.

They're tired of politicans who break promises, business-men who cheat, evangelists who exploit, journalists who distort, military leaders who waste tax dollars, and labor officials who keep demanding more.

Many Americans are skeptical about the same institutions and leadership that used to engender automatic allegiance from their grandparents. In fact, the number of people expressing a great deal of confidence in various institutions—including Congress, the executive branch, schools, the military, the media, and organized labor—declined markedly between 1973 and 1989.

But the biggest deterioration has been in attitudes toward organized religion. The number of Americans expressing a lot of confidence in religious institutions dropped 55% during those years. By 1989, only about one in five people would admit to having considerable confidence in organized religion.[1]

"Americans believe, across the board, that our current political, religious, and business leaders have failed us miserably and completely," wrote James Patterson and Peter Kim in *The Day America Told the Truth.*"[2]

Or as Church Lady lamented on *Saturday Night Live*: "We're living in trying times—everybody's trying everything and getting caught!"

But all is not lost. Consider this point:

Observation #9: Harry may distrust authority, but he's receptive to authentic biblical leadership.

You see, the same shortcomings that have turned off Americans to major national institutions—deceit, greed, arrogance, self-promotion, and abuse of power—are also the antithesis of biblical leadership. And when Unchurched Harry sees the opposite values being lived out in a church's leadership, there's a good chance that he won't paint those leaders with the same brush of disdain.

Chances are that he'll respond positively to those who are accountable and open in their financial dealings; moderate in their lifestyle; humble in their demeanor; modest about their achievements and who use their influence to serve people in need.

In other words, leaders who follow Christ's example. Jesus was the consummate leader, and He exhibited unfailing humility. He said that He "did not come to be served, but to serve,"[3] and He lived out that value by washing the feet of His disciples and even going to the Cross to pay for our sins.

"The cultivation of love and its mood—humility—is essential for the Christlike leader because they are characteristics not often found among so-called leaders who are not Christlike," said leadership expert John Haggai. He said leaders should "follow Christ's example in personal relationships by avoiding elitism, intolerance, class distinction, and self-promotion."[4]

Generally, Harry prefers down-to-earth, straight-talking leaders, ones who don't insist on "Doctor" or "Reverend" before their names, who don't have a personalized parking space in a prime location, who don't insist on perks, and who aren't setting themselves apart by wearing robes on Sundays. To many Harrys, especially baby boomers and busters, those trappings smack of elitism and, in some cases, arrogance.

And, by the way, Harry isn't just scrutinizing "professional" ministers. If you're serving as a lay leader in your church, he's got his eyes on you, too. He wants to see if you're any different from those haughty leaders in other sectors of society. If you're not, you'll be giving him one more excuse to steer clear of church.

But biblical leaders—those who lead out of a desire to serve—will not only attract Harry, they might even inspire him.

Observation #10: Harry is no longer loyal to denominations, but he is attracted to places where his needs will be met.

Since I've been married, I've owned a Toyota, Nissan, Chrysler, Chevy, Mazda, Oldsmobile, Volkswagen, and, I'm sorry to say, that aesthetic embarrassment—the American Motors Pacer. (Yes, the same model that Wayne and Garth drove in *Wayne's World*.)

When it comes to cars, I don't care about the make or model as much as I'm concerned about getting a vehicle that meets my needs at a price I can afford. Even when the government was chiding everybody to buy American, I was still tempted to buy a Japanese model because it was best suited for me.

Madison Avenue has been saying for years that in this consumer-dominated culture, the day of brand loyalty is largely gone. Now denominational loyalty is faltering, too.

Among the twenty reasons that church consultant Lyle Schaller cites for declining denominational allegiance are:

• The sharp increase in interfaith marriages since 1945;

• The rise of ecumenicalism, which has made denominations seem archaic;

• The shedding of old loyalties as people have become upwardly mobile;

• The decision by some denominational leaders to make public pronouncements that have alienated members;

• The denominational mergers since 1950 and the failure to engender new loyalties;

• The proliferation of parachurch organizations that "catch the allegiance of members of denominations that may not offer anything equally appealing."

• The emergence of high-visibility independent churches that offer high-quality programs.[5]

Today, Unchurched Harry is a comparison shopper, even in the spiritual arena. The fact that he was confirmed as a Lutheran may still exert some influence in which church he will try first when he's ready to return, but foremost on his mind are issues of quality, creativity, and relevance to his felt needs. If he finds them elsewhere, that's where he probably will go.

He's even willing to jump from one denomination to another and back from week to week in order to take advantage of specific programs that offer him practical help for his day-to-day living. Ten percent of adults are church-hopping like that today; by the year 2000, one person in four may be dividing his or her loyalty and giving.[6]

Lately I've noticed an increasing animosity among unchurched people toward the idea of denominations. They seem to see their existence as an illustration of divisiveness within the larger church. Some see the concept of a distant headquarters exerting control over a local congregation to be analogous to Congress dictating to cities—and you know how people feel about Congress these days!

I try to stay away from denominational issues when I'm relating to an unchurched person. Instead of having him compare the doctrinal stands of various denominations as some Harrys want to do, I urge him to determine what the Bible teaches and then to select a church whose beliefs are consistent with that. That tends to keep him on track with the big picture instead of getting bogged down in less significant doctrinal nuances.

Here are some implications for denominational churches in reaching Unchurched Harry:

• Don't count on an appeal to his dormant denominational ties in order to get him back to church. He'll respond much better to an invitation to a specific program or event that will meet his needs.

• Churches should consider dropping the denominational affiliation from their name in certain instances. For example, while the Baptist name may be a draw in the South, where 45% of the residents have a very favorable impression of that denomination, it's a deterrent in the Rocky Mountain states, where only 6% are very positive toward it.

The Lutheran church carries only an 8% "very favorable" rating in the South but 21% in the Midwest. The Presbyterian name doesn't score well among singles or young people; the Methodist title fares better in predominantly black areas than Hispanic.[7]

Some denominational churches have started using "community church" in their titles, which is generally well-received by Harry since it suggests local involvement and community ties.

• Denominations should guard against reliance on traditional modes of ministry and instead free up members to pioneer cutting-edge programs tailored to Harry's specific needs. Entrepreneurial individuals should be given resources and sufficient autonomy to plant new congregations where they can experiment with different paradigms for reaching Harry.

• Local churches should be encouraged to understand the

Unchurched Harry in their own backyards so they can respond quickly and accurately to his needs rather than relying on cues from the denominational hierarchy.

• Traditional congregations should be nudged toward being more "seeker friendly" in their worship and to develop appropriate periodic outreach events and special services where their members can bring unchurched friends.

• Blurring the line between laity and "professional" ministers would be a positive development to Harry, who is rankled by "elitism" and generally believes in grass-roots involvement in organizations.

• Values that attract Unchurched Harry—such as excellence, creativity, authenticity, relevance, meaningful participation by the laity, and servant leadership—should be modeled and facilitated from the top of the denominational structure.

• The attitude, "That's the way we've always done things" needs to become, "What can we do better to meet more needs and reach more people with the Gospel?"

Observation #11: Harry isn't much of a joiner, but he's hungry for a cause he can connect with.

The year was 1983, and Steve Jobs, the hard-driving visionary behind Apple Computers, needed a world-class executive to take over the day-to-day helm of his burgeoning company.

In a question that has gone down in business history, he looked Pepsi-Cola executive John Scully square in the eyes and asked: "Do you want to spend the rest of your life selling sugared water, or do you want a chance to change the world?" Scully signed up to change the world.[8]

There are millions of Unchurched Harrys who want to change the world, too. They want to leave a mark. They want to make a difference. They were inspired when John Kennedy said, "Ask not what your country can do for you; ask what you can do for your country." Their spirits resonated when Martin Luther King, Jr., declared, "I have a dream."

That's especially true of baby boomers, many of whom were involved with the anti-war and racial integration movements of the 1960s. Despite bouts of disillusionment since then, their idealistic streak largely remains intact.

They're hungry for a cause that they can believe in. When pollsters asked Americans whether they'd be willing to give up two weeks a year to tackle some of the country's most serious problems, nearly six out of ten said, "sign me up."[9]

"The 1990s will be marked by very personalized moral crusades," predicted James Patterson and Peter Kim, citing the environmental movement as the first example. "Many of us ache to do the right thing, but we feel that there are no sane outlets through our institutions."[10]

A significant number of Unchurched Harrys would return to church if they thought it would be an institution through which meaningful social change could be accomplished. In fact, when unchurched people were asked what would attract them, the second most common answer (after better preaching) was for the church to become more involved in its community.

"People mentioned social activism as a key function of the church: helping the poor and needy, offering education, attacking prejudice and oppression, providing financial and material relief to victims of disaster, etc.," said George Barna, who conducted the study.[11]

George Gallup's survey found that nearly one out of five unchurched people said they would come to a church that was "serious about working for a better society."[12]

Actually, it's a great fit. Jesus taught His followers to provide for the needy, stick up for the downtrodden, and oppose oppression, and Harry is saying that's an agenda that could attract him to church. While Harry's motivations might be tainted—his main purpose in helping others may stem from a selfish desire to feel good about himself—at least he's willing to participate. And if he does, this kind of social action provides a way to communicate biblical values and the Gospel to him.

When a church sponsors social action projects, such as refurbishing homes for the poor or feeding the hungry at Thanksgiving, it creates an excellent opportunity for you to invite along the appropriate kind of unchurched friend. Working side-by-side to make a difference in the lives of hurting people offers a terrific environment for talking about what's really important in life.

While Harry might be willing to sign up for a cause, however, he's less likely to sign up with an institution. There's an aversion—again, mostly among younger people—to formally joining anything.

"We baby boomers aren't coming to church to become members," said one pastor, himself a boomer. "We're coming to *experience* something. Yes, even to *get* something."[13]

As for baby busters, "They have learned to live with change and endless choices. They are reluctant to make firm commitments lest they overlook something or make a mistake."[14]

For some unchurched people, the idea of church membership strikes them as negative. In his cynical moments, Harry wonders, *Why do they want my name on a roster somewhere—so they can brag about how many members they have?* Besides, most churches aren't like American Express, where "membership has its privileges." So the attitude becomes, why join?

Churches should expect a long, slow courtship by Unchurched Harry, followed by difficulty in consummating the relationship. He may serve in a church, give to a church, and participate in a church long before he's willing to make a formal commitment to God or the church itself.

Church leaders can adjust to this phenomenon by opening up as many opportunities as possible for participation by people who aren't formal members. Once Harry comes through the door, let him get involved in appropriate areas as much as he wants as he moves toward making the most important commitment of all, which is to Christ.

Observation #12: Even if Harry's not spiritually sensitive, he wants his children to get quality moral training.

Our phone rang one day and my daughter Alison answered it. I heard her politely provide the times for our weekend outreach services and then hang up.

"Who was that?" I asked.

"Mr. Johnson," she replied.

I was astounded! I knew Bill Johnson (not his real name) from my days as a newspaperman. Though I had shared my faith with him and tried repeatedly to interest him in coming to church with me, he had always found excuses not to go, but we had maintained a relationship through the years. In fact, Alison sometimes babysat for his daughter.

"Why was he asking about church services?" I asked.

"He said he thought it was time that his daughter Meghan got some religious training," Alison told me. "So they're going to visit this weekend."

This was the latest illustration of something I've never quite figured out. Regardless of the level of Unchurched Harry's spiritual interest, despite his own dissatisfaction with the church, what draws him back is his feeling many times that his children need some religious training.

When researchers interviewed five hundred people between the ages of thirty-three and forty-two who had been confirmed as Presbyterians in the 1950s and 1960s, they found that about half were now unchurched. Yet while they've abandoned the church themselves, they "still believe the church has a valid role in promoting a 'moral code' for society and would like their children to have some form of religious education."[15]

In another study, 55% of unchurched baby boomer men said they definitely have no plans to join a church in the next five years—but 73% of them said they want their children to get religious training.[16] Another sampling found that 48% of unchurched parents already have their children enrolled for religious instruction.[17]

I'm not exactly sure what drives this seemingly contradictory phenomenon. Maybe some parents merely feel, "If I had to go through confirmation when I was a kid, then my kids should, too." Or maybe parents have suffered the fallout from the mistakes they made during the drug-and-sex '60s, and they want to spare their children the same pain by giving them some moral guidance. Perhaps they think that some religious input will help inoculate their kids from AIDS and other modern hazards of loose living.

In any event, this trend offers two excellent opportunities. First, it's a chance to reach these youngsters with the Gospel, since children are more open than their parents to spiritual matters. In fact, about two-thirds of all commitments to Christ are made by people under eighteen.[18]

And, second, it's an opportunity to impact their parents. This can be an especially good way to make inroads in the hard-to-reach category of college graduates. Studies have shown that parents with college degrees are more likely than those with less education to seek religious training for their kids.[19]

If Unchurched Harry and Mary see a youth program that's relevant, dynamic, and staffed by people who have an authentic faith, they're going to be more likely to explore what adult programs the church provides.

I know two parents who are coming to our church only because their six-year-old son enjoys the youth ministry so much. "About Wednesday or Thursday, he starts asking if we're going to church on Sunday," the mother said. "He doesn't stop until I tell him yes." While he's with kids in his age group, the parents are in the adult service, and they're starting to grow spiritually.

The challenge, though, is to provide the kind of quality children's program that today's parents expect. Sesame Street and Disney World have set high standards in the minds of today's consumers.

In fact, this is disheartening: only one out of three church-going adults rate their own church's ministry for children as being excellent.[20] If church people aren't sold on their own program, then chances are Harry and Mary won't be either.

Any church intent on reaching Unchurched Harry and Mary should honestly assess their youth program, examining it through the grid of the unchurched mindset. The critical factor is who's running the ministry. If the church relies on the old-fashioned method of staffing its Sunday school—with the pastor brow-beating members into doing their stint so that bedlam won't break out among the kids—the program will never thrive.

However, when the church helps people discover their spiritual gifts, unlock what they're passionate about, and determine their temperament type, and then funnels people into children's ministry who are designed by God for that very purpose, watch out! All the church has to do is give them enough freedom to create their own world for the kids.

One caution: Unchurched children are quite a bit different from children who have grown up in Christian homes. Any youth program should be sensitive to the embarrassment and confusion that these kids feel when they don't understand the Christian subculture or lingo.

In other words, just as outreach services for adults have to be adjusted for Unchurched Harry and Mary, the Sunday school needs to be revamped for little Unchurched Gary and Sheri.

Observation #13: Harry and Mary are confused about sex roles, but they don't know that the Bible can clarify for them what it means to be a man and woman.

Recent trends in society have left Unchurched Harry bewildered about what masculinity is. Should his role models be Phil Donahue and Alan Alda, or Sylvester Stallone and Arnold Schwarzenegger? He feels whipsawed between the women's movement that's urging him to be more sensitive and the men's movement that's advising him to get back to his primal roots.

To sort through it all, some business executives are going on men's retreats in the country, where . . .

They dress like wanna-be savages and hunch over steaming rocks in makeshift "sweat lodges." Banging goatskin drums to an uneven rhythm, they wail like fatted calves ready for the slaughter.

These men, we are told, lead lives of quiet desperation. Each day, they butt heads with an unfriendly society that has stripped them of their masculinity. By pouring out their hearts—and buckets of perspiration—to each other, they emerge from the sweat lodges with their manhood restored.

At least, that's the game plan.[21]

Unfortunately, one of the last places that Harry thinks to look for insight on his manhood is the church, and yet that's exactly where real answers can be found. The role model that Harry is searching for is Jesus Christ, who embodies the masculine ideal. As University of Colorado football coach Bill McCartney says, "A man's man is a godly man."[22]

When churches begin to speak from the Bible in relevant and practical terms about sex roles, it will strike a responsive chord in Harry. At one seeker-oriented church, four of the ten most popular messages in 1991 dealt with clarifying male and female issues. After a message titled, "What is a Man?" one out of five people stopped to purchase an instant cassette tape so they could rehear the sermon or pass it on to someone else.[23]

At Cherry Hills Community Church near Denver, executive pastor Bob Beltz started meeting with six men on Tuesday mornings in 1980 to discuss biblical masculinity. By 1992, more than 300 men packed the 7:00 A.M. get-togethers to talk about the topic. "We just can't fit anybody else in the room," Beltz said.[24]

Churches interested in attracting Harry should consider

what programs, including group discussions and topical Bible studies, they could start to help him clarify what it means to be a man of the '90s. Also, individual Christians should be alert in their relationships with unchurched men for opportunities to point them toward Jesus as being the ultimate example of well-balanced manhood.

Meanwhile, Unchurched Mary is grappling with her own sexual identity. Often, she's doing an exhausting juggling act, trying to balance marriage, family, and a career. Feminists are shouting in one ear, "You can have it all," while her churched friends are whispering with disdain in the other, "A mother's place should be at home with her kids."

Like Harry, Mary doesn't think of looking to the church for answers. Her mental image of a typical Women's Ministry is that it's not "her kind of people." It would probably be geared more toward homemaking issues than career topics, and she'd walk away feeling more guilty than ever about working outside her home.

Besides, she may believe that churches have always been a male-dominated institution where women are kept from key decision-making positions. To her, that just shows how out of touch they are.

Mary needs to see churches that are addressing her felt needs and relating to her world. For instance, ministries specially geared for working women are becoming increasingly popular. But equally important in helping Mary understand what it means to be a woman is for her to see churches where women have access to leadership and influence.

As the apostle Paul wrote, "There is neither Jew nor Greek, slave nor free, male nor female, for you are all one in Christ Jesus."[25] Of course, if that were the *only* verse that Paul penned on the topic of women, there wouldn't be any controversy. As it is, churches are divided over the appropriate role of women in leadership and teaching.

It's important to emphasize that our effort to make the

church more attractive to Unchurched Mary should never prompt us to disregard or violate biblical imperatives. However, I'm convinced that a fair and balanced reading of Scripture discloses that women are eligible to teach, lead, and participate in every aspect of ministry. For an excellent analysis of biblical teaching on the topic, I'd suggest Dr. Gilbert Bilezikian's book, *Beyond Sex Roles*.[26]

So it's not on the basis of expediency that I believe churches should open up their leadership ranks to women; it's on the basis of biblical authority. And as Unchurched Mary sorts through what it means to be a woman of the '90s, she will be much more willing to seek help from a church that endorses her access to full participation.

Observation #14: Harry is proud that he's tolerant of different faiths, but he thinks Christians are narrow-minded.

Perhaps the most controversial statement made by Jesus Christ was when He declared: "I am the way and the truth and the life. No one comes to the Father except through me."[27] It's that claim of Christ's exclusivity that rankles Unchurched Harry.

Harry is willing to let Christians worship their God, Muslims worship Allah, and Hindus worship their proliferation of gods. But when Christians assert that their way is the *only* way to heaven, Harry calls that bigotry.

After all, aren't there many roads that lead to God? Don't all religions teach the universal brotherhood of man? How can Christians be so snobbish as to believe that they're right and everybody else is wrong?

When the *New Age Journal* published an article on how parents talk to their children about God, it ran side-by-side stories of Jewish, Catholic, Neo-pagan, and Zen Buddhist families.[28] There were no value judgments on which faith was right or wrong. That's certainly the '90s way—all opinions about God are equally valid because every belief is a slice of the same reality.

What bothers Harry is that Christians balk at playing by the same rules. Surveys have shown that only a small percentage of unchurched people think that churches are tolerant of people with different ideas.[29]

Some of Harry's notions about the equal value of various religions stems from a misunderstanding of the U.S. Constitution, which guarantees that every religious system has freedom of expression and equal protection under the law.

"Though the concept of legal religious toleration says nothing at all about the validity of truth claims, many have drawn the implication that equal toleration means equal validity," R. C. Sproul said. "Thus, when Christians. . . make claims of exclusivity, their claims are often met with shock or anger at such a narrow-minded posture."[30]

Often, Unchurched Harry reacts to Christ the way the young Hindu man did when I told him about Jesus during a trip to India in 1987. When he heard me say that Jesus is God, he replied, "No problem."

"No problem?" I said with surprise. "You're saying that you accept the fact that Jesus Christ is the Son of God?"

"Sure," he replied. I was amazed he had agreed to my premise so readily. But then he added: "We have millions of gods in Hinduism. We'll be glad to add Jesus as one more."

When I asserted that Jesus is the *only* Son of God, that's when he got indignant. And the same is true of many Unchurched Harrys. Jesus is fine with them as long as He's just one option among many.

Christians need to be careful about the way they explain Christ's exclusivity claim to Harry. The danger, of course, is sounding smug or superior. Actually, as someone once said, Christians shouldn't be snobbish; we're just beggars telling other beggars where to find food.

Sometimes, to defuse Harry's objections, I use an analogy of two country clubs. The first club only lets in people who have earned their membership. They must have accomplished something, obtained superior wisdom, or fulfilled a list of demands and requirements before they're considered for admission. Despite their efforts, many people just won't make the grade and will be turned away.

That's what every other religion is like, because they're all based on the system of people doing something to earn God's favor.

But the second country club says, "Anybody who wants in can come in. Men, women, black, white, old, young—whoever seeks entrance can have it through repentance and faith in Christ. We won't turn anyone away who asks to come in, but we'll leave it up to you whether you want to join."

That's what Christianity is saying. So, which belief system is snobbish and exclusive? Our door is open to anyone who wants to come in.

Then I try to get Harry to consider the logic of Christ's exclusivity claim. In other words, it wouldn't make sense that God would go over to one side of the world and tell people how to please Him, then go to another place and tell people something conflicting, and go elsewhere and give another story. God isn't schizophrenic. It defies logic to say that religions with contradictory beliefs about God could all be right at the same time.

After that I discuss the credentials of Christ, which are unlike any other religious leader's. I talk about how He authenticated His claims through numerous miracles, the fulfillment of prophecy against all odds, and His resurrection— all seen by many people and recorded by eyewitnesses. Those credentials make His claims credible.

By this time, Harry often is willing to shelve his objection that Christians are narrow-minded—at least for a while until he can examine the claims of Christ in more detail.

Observation #15: There's a good chance Harry would try church if a friend invited him—but this may actually do him more harm than good.

The statistic is stunning.

A national survey by Barna Research found that one out of four unchurched people would gladly attend church if a friend would only extend an invitation.[31]

This means on any given Sunday morning, 14 to 20 million adults are sitting home because nobody took the simple step of asking them to attend a church service. Twenty million people are as many as in New York City, Los Angeles, Chicago, Houston, Philadelphia, Detroit, San Diego, and San Francisco put together!

Can you imagine what would happen if we really got serious about evangelism and invited all those people to church one Sunday? The pews would be packed!

That's the power of the relational pull. You see, when a Christian builds an authentic friendship with Unchurched Harry, he's developing credibility with him. It only makes sense that Harry would be willing to give church a try if his trusted friend encouraged him. That's especially true if the friend's life reflects a transformation that's attributable to Christ. As my colleague Mark Mittelberg, a former electronics salesman, likes to point out, "Friends buy from friends."

And yet, unfortunately, there's a downside to this statistic. One in four unchurched people may give church a try, *but what will they find when they get there?*

Remember, most unchurched people used to attend church regularly.[32] They stopped going for a reason. Often, that reason was that services were boring, predictable, irrelevant, and they felt that the church was always going after their money.

So what happens when Unchurched Harry returns and finds that little or nothing has changed? The danger is that he'll soon get fed up again and leave once more—and next time it's going to be even more difficult to convince him to give the church one more try.

Alarmingly, that's what is starting to happen. A few years ago, the headlines in the Christian media were jubilant:

• *Baby Boomers Rediscover Church*

- *A Generation Warms to Religion*
- *The Boomers Are Back!*[33]

Sociologists speculated that boomers were repeating a pattern seen in the past: After they reach a certain life stage of responsibility, increased conservatism, and parenthood, they begin to think about going back to the church they had left years earlier.

But more recent statistics are showing that the boomers may have come in the church's front door, checked out what was going on, and are now exiting the back door once more.

In March 1992, the periodical *Ministry Currents* first reported that the number of baby boomers attending church dropped from 50% in 1991 to 40% in 1992—a decline that was attributed to an increasing number of adults finding the local church "irrelevant to their everyday life."[34]

"This decline cannot be explained away by sampling error, given the number of boomers who were interviewed," said George Barna, whose firm conducted the study. "Since boomers are among those leading the cadre of adults who charge that local churches tend to be irrelevant, this possibility of a generational retreat from the church must be taken seriously."[35]

Whether or not this trend continues, it should be a wake-up call to the American church. The time has come for a renewed partnership to be forged between the church and its members.

Individual Christians need to rededicate themselves to praying and fasting for Unchurched Harry and Mary, building authentic relationships with them, sharing the Gospel with them, answering their questions, and inviting them to church.

At the same time, churches need to assist their members by creating services or outreach events that will meaningfully connect with the unchurched mindset.

The failure to work together in fulfilling the Great Commission would be a costly mistake. And yet when the church and its members strategically work in tandem, the return on our investment of prayer, effort, and risk-taking will be incredibly rich.

6
MEETING HARRY
WHERE HE LIVES

It was a beautiful Sunday afternoon in California's Santa Ana Mountains when Susan Small and her five-year-old daughter, Laura, wandered down to a pond to watch tadpoles dart around the murky water.

Suddenly, a mountain lion sprang from the bushes and pounced on Laura, knocking her down, grabbing her head in its mouth, and dragging her away into the thick underbrush. They disappeared before Mrs. Small could even manage to scream: "The lion has my child!"

About two hundred yards away, a hiker named Greg Ysais heard the cry and came running. Without hesitating, he plunged through the bushes in search for the child—and instantly came face-to-face with the growling mountain lion, which was holding little Laura by the neck.

Greg had to think quickly. He tore a small limb from a

dead tree and advanced toward the animal, yelling and trying to poke it in the eye. The mountain lion growled and swatted at him. For several tense moments, there was a stand-off. Would the enraged lion rip Laura apart? Would it lunge for Greg?

Slowly, the animal loosened its grip on the child, and her limp body dropped to the ground. It looked as if the lion was going to attack Greg, but he kept fending it off with the branch. Finally, the mountain lion turned and fled into the bushes, and Mrs. Small rushed over to pick up her child, who was injured but still alive. Gregory Ysais, a thirty-six-year-old electronics technician, was a hero. In almost a reflexive reaction, he made a heroic choice to save that child. And Mrs. Small's grateful response was understandable. "We'll never forget what Gregory Ysais did for us," she said.[1]

What qualities does Greg Ysais share with other heroes whose stories we read about in the newspaper—the ones who save babies from burning buildings, rescue motorists from mangled cars, and venture into deep waters to reach struggling swimmers?

They are all ordinary people who came to a critical turning point and made an extraordinary decision to rescue someone whose life was in danger. And most often, that involved putting themselves in peril.

By the same token, as a Bible-believing follower of Jesus Christ, I know there's a literal life-and-death battle being waged all around me every day. You feel that, too, don't you? You know that some people in your neighborhood, your office, or even in your family are in jeopardy of facing eternal death—and they probably don't even realize they need to be rescued.

Almost every day, we come to evangelistic turning points. We make choices whether to help rescue these people from danger or to walk the other way. We make spur-of-the-moment decisions whether to heroically venture into their lives and lead them to a place of spiritual safety, or to merely hope that someone else will do it.

Jesus constantly faced those same kinds of turning points. Looking at one scene from His life will illustrate five of them and will give us insights on reaching the Unchurched Harrys and Marys in our own lives.

The Pharisees heard that Jesus was gaining and baptizing more disciples than John, although in fact it was not Jesus who baptized, but his disciples. When the Lord learned of this, He left Judea and went back once more to Galilee.

Now he had to go through Samaria. So he came to a town in Samaria called Sychar, near the plot of ground Jacob had given to his son Joseph. Jacob's well was there, and Jesus, tired as he was from the journey, sat down by the well. It was about the sixth hour.[2]

This episode takes place rather early in Jesus' ministry. He was already attracting attention from religious leaders, and because He didn't want to clash with them yet, He left for Galilee.

Did you notice that the writer says Jesus "had to go through Samaria." If you look at a map, you might say, "Well, of course, if someone were going to travel from Judea to Galilee, he'd probably take a short-cut through Samaria. After all, Samaria is sandwiched between them." But sometimes the most logical route isn't the most-traveled path.

In fact, that's not the route that strict Jews typically took. Usually, a devout Jew traveling toward Galilee would skirt Samaria by crossing the Jordan River and taking the longer way. The reason was simple: Samaritans inhabited Samaria, and there was cultural, ethnic, religious, and political animosity between the Jews and Samaritans.

Even today, people avoid going through neighborhoods that are inhabited by people who differ from them. Some whites are hesitant to travel through predominantly black areas; there are blacks who choose routes that take them around white enclaves. They avoid interaction because they don't feel at ease among folks who are different.

But Jesus decided to travel *through* Samaria. In fact, the Bible emphasizes that He "had to" take that route—not for practical reasons, but for a spiritual purpose. He came to a turning point and made the divine decision that He was going to break down barriers of prejudice and mistrust. Some even see Jesus' route as a protest against the stubborn refusal of the Pharisees to mix with people beyond their faith. So Jesus' decision demonstrates the first insight:

• **Rescuing people in spiritual peril frequently requires us to strategically venture into their environment.**

That can be uncomfortable for Christians. We'd rather distance ourselves from the unpleasant environment where Unchurched Harry and Mary live. I remember seeing footage of our troops digging foxholes in the sands of Kuwait before Operation Desert Storm. I thought, *That's what Christians are like sometimes.* Many people who become Christians are so glad to escape from the ugliness of the world that they dig figurative foxholes so they can huddle together in safety.

Let's admit it: It's far more enjoyable to hang around with Christians than non-believers. We worship the same God, we share the same values, and we speak the same language. We don't blister each other's ears with dirty language or subject each other to the hazards of secondhand cigarette smoke. And so we gravitate more and more toward people like ourselves.

But Jesus maintained balance in His life. He had what has been called a "macro-ministry," an over-arching mission from God to reach the world, and He also regularly engaged in "micro-ministry," which means getting to know and befriend lost people, one at a time. For us, though, sometimes it's difficult to keep our equilibrium.

I know I've fallen out of balance on occasion. I had an old school friend who moved back to the Chicago area a few years ago, and we got together a couple of times. While he seemed somewhat receptive to spiritual discussions, it was clear that I was going to have to rebuild our friendship before I could earn the right to delve deeply into such a personal topic as God.

But I was so busy in my "macro-ministry" at the church, doing all kinds of worthwhile activities to further the cause of Christ on a broad scale, that I never got around to investing time in the "micro-ministry" of our friendship.

Then one day he called. "My company's transferring me back to the West Coast," he said. "I'm leaving right away."

I had missed an opportunity because I hadn't been as intentional as Jesus in purposefully venturing into the environment of non-believers and building relationships with them.

Actually, there are lots of ways we can strategically enter into the world of Unchurched Harry and Mary. We can patronize the same shops, restaurants, and gas stations instead of always changing to new ones, so that we get to know the salespeople, waiters and waitresses, and attendants. Although our church has a place where I can purchase lunch on campus, I still eat regularly at a small café because I've been building a relationship with the owners.

We can join park district softball leagues instead of segregating ourselves in church leagues. We can become active in civic and school organizations so we can continue to develop social contacts with unchurched people.

One effective strategy is to specifically work at retaining contact with some of the unchurched friends you had before you became a committed Christian. I've maintained contacts with several journalists with whom I used to work, and I try to regularly venture onto their turf to keep up our relationship in the hopes that I can influence them for Christ.

But if your non-Christian friendships have faded because your new church relationships keep you too busy, here's a suggestion: revisit their environment and re-establish a connection with one or two of your former buddies. Call up the person you used to hit the bars with and say, "You know, I've missed seeing you. Let's get together—except let's have lunch this time."

Of course, you have to guard against situations where you'll be tempted to slip back into the behavior that typified your pre-Christian days. But what makes this approach so effective is that old friends—and even old acquaintances who weren't particularly close friends—are amazingly receptive to reestablishing contact.

I remember a college friend who disappeared from my life after we went our separate ways at graduation. Yet when I telephoned him a while back, we were chatting like old buddies after just a few minutes. Even though he lives in another part of the country, we've made an effort to get together a few times since then, and he has taken dramatic steps in his spiritual journey.

There are some definite advantages to this approach. Because you used to be friends, you already know there will be some affinity between you. And this renewed relationship will open up all sorts of natural opportunities for you to talk, over the long haul, about the changes you've experienced in your life since coming to Christ. After all, what's going to be a main topic of conversation? It's going to be what's been happening in each other's lives. What a great chance to talk about the impact Christ has had on you!

A while ago I ventured back into my old environment at the federal courthouse in Chicago, where I used to work as a reporter, and I ran into a crusty old newsman whom I knew before I became a Christian.

He stuck out his hand and said enthusiastically, "So, Strobel, how the (blank) are you, you old son of a (blank). I haven't seen you in a long time! What the (blank) have you been doing lately? You still at the (blanking) *Tribune*?"

I said, "Well, I've had a lot of change in my life. In fact, I work at a church now."

His cigarette almost fell out of his mouth. "I'll be damned!" he said.

"Well," I chuckled, "you don't have to be."

That opened the door to a spiritual conversation, and I'm praying that our renewed relationship will give me future opportunities to talk to him about Christ.

So where's your Samaria? What strategic choice can you make to enter an unbeliever's enclave and connect with him or her for the eventual purpose of doing kingdom business?

Of course, there are risks. There's always a risk when you do something heroic, and the risk here is to your reputation as a Christian. If you're seen hanging around with people who are known to be living ungodly lifestyles, what will your churched friends think of you?

Once I was walking down the street with a reporter friend of mine, and while we were deep in a spiritual conversation, we passed a dirty, smoke-filled tavern. "C'mon in here; let's talk about this some more," he said, tugging me by the arm. As I sat at a small table talking about God, I wondered what someone from my church would think if they were walking by and saw me inside.

Then I remembered that Jesus was a "friend of tax collectors and sinners," and He interacted with them so much that He was mistakenly accused of being a glutton and a drunkard.[3] He wasn't compromised by the world, but He did enter into the world to get alongside spiritually hurting people. After all, how can you rescue other people unless you get close to them?

Now let's continue replaying the scene from Jesus' life as He comes upon His second turning point:

When a Samaritan woman came to draw water, Jesus said to her, "Will you give me a drink?" (His disciples had gone into the town to buy food.)

The Samaritan woman said to him, "You are a Jew and I am a Samaritan woman. How can you ask me for a drink?" (For Jews do not associate with Samaritans.)[4]

Jesus encountered a woman at the well, and He had a few options. One would have been to supernaturally satisfy His thirst. If Jesus could feed multitudes of people with just a few fish and loaves of bread, He certainly could have miraculously satisfied His own need for water. Or He could make the effort to initiate a conversation that just might lead into spiritual territory. Jesus chose to make contact with the woman, and so our second insight reads:

• Often, before we can be used to rescue someone from spiritual danger, we have to build a relational bridge to them.

That's what Jesus did in short order. While it may not seem that asking for a drink of water would be very effective in reaching out to the woman, in that culture those few words packed a powerful punch. Just by starting a conversation with a Samaritan woman, Jesus was tearing down huge social barriers because normally a Jew wouldn't even drink from a Samaritan's water bucket.

Instead of shunning her, Jesus used six well-chosen words to demonstrate acceptance of her. He opened a relational door by communicating that she mattered to Him and that she had dignity as a person. You can see by her reaction that His approach was effective; she was shocked that Jesus would even talk to her.

There are lots of times when we come across this kind of evangelistic turning point and we make choices whether or not we're going to initiate contact with a spiritually starved person. While we're taking a walk around the block, we can stop to meet the new neighbor who's washing his car, or we can stroll on by. We can choose to linger for a few moments and get to know the clerk at the dry cleaners, or we can dash home. We can invite a business colleague to lunch, or we can eat our meals with Christians. How many times do we rush past opportunities to make relational inroads with unbelievers?

After all, building a relational bridge to another person isn't very difficult, especially when you know the key: *listening to the other person.* It's taking a genuine interest in Unchurched Harry's life. It's asking him questions. It's finding out about his world. It's expressing authentic curiosity about his situation in life.

When you do that, many times you'll discover some common interests that you can use to deepen the relationship. And at the same time, you're doing what Jesus did with the woman at the well: you're affirming Harry's value and dignity just by taking the time to sincerely relate to him.

Is there someone in your world for whom you could make a choice to build a relational bridge? Maybe it's the person who just joined your company and is feeling like an outsider. Or the cashier you see at the health club when you stop by to work out every Wednesday evening. Or the fellow student at those MBA classes you're taking on weekends. Or the mechanic at the service station who always seems to be working on your car.

As for Jesus, He made a point to build a brief friendship with the woman at the well, but He wasn't content just to engage in small talk. Let's continue to play out that scene:

Jesus answered her, "If you knew the gift of God and who it is that asks you for a drink, you would have asked him and he would have given you living water."

"Sir," the woman said, "you have nothing to draw with and the well is deep. Where can you get this living water? Are you greater than our father Jacob, who gave us the well and drank from it himself, as did also his sons and his flocks and herds?"

Jesus answered, "Everybody who drinks this water will be thirsty again, but whoever drinks the water I give him will never thirst. Indeed, the water I give him will become in him a spring of water welling up to everlasting life."

The woman said to him, "Sir, give me this water so that I won't get thirsty and have to keep coming here to draw water . . ."[5]

As the scene continues, the Scriptures report:

The woman said, "I know that Messiah" (called Christ) "is coming. When he comes, he will explain everything to us." Then Jesus declared, "I who speak to you am he."[6]

Jesus had just come to a third turning point and made another split-second spiritual decision, and it's a critically important one. He decided He would turn the conversation from the routine to the spiritual because He knew:

• **To successfully rescue someone, at some point we have to clearly point out the path to safety.**

Friends, it's imperative that we get into a spiritual discussion and eventually point Unchurched Harry or Mary toward Christ as being the only hope for rescue. Jesus made a conscious choice to steer His conversation into spiritual territory, and we can learn from the way He did it.

For instance, He didn't spout a canned speech or recite a memorized presentation. He didn't launch into a tirade or condemn her. He didn't even begin quoting Scripture right off the bat. Instead, He took advantage of the circumstances that they found themselves in—they were talking about water, so He used "living water" as an analogy for God.

He piqued her curiosity. He unfolded His message slowly and at a pace at which she could take it in. He tailored His presentation to who she was, what she was like, and what she knew about.

This is the turning point where most of us get tripped up, isn't it? We're not sure how to turn an everyday conversation to spiritual matters in a natural way. And, again, do you know what the key is? *It's listening,* because when we really listen and get to know another person, we'll come across natural opportunities to maneuver the conversation into spiritual topics.

For instance, when you find out Unchurched Mary has a couple of children who are driving her crazy, you could play it safe and say, "I know what you're saying; my kids drive me up the wall sometimes, too." Or, you can make a split-second decision to say, "You know, my kids can be a handful, but I was amazed to find out that the Bible has some great advice for raising kids. It's really helped me." That opens the door to a spiritual discussion, and maybe you could even follow it up by lending her a Christian book about parenting.

Or if you discover that Unchurched Harry suffers from a sagging self-esteem, you can make a split-second decision to say, "I get down on myself sometimes, too, but you know what? A while back I found out something that changed my whole attitude about myself. Let me know if you want to hear about it sometime." You've probably raised his curiosity, and when he's ready to ask you to explain, you can tell him how your own self-esteem has soared ever since you learned how much you matter to God.

Bill Hybels has suggested a natural way for executives to steer conversations into spiritual territory. A common question among people in business is, "How's your year going?" The reply is usually something like, "Not bad; how's yours?" But the reply could be: "My business life is doing well, my family life is doing great, and my spiritual life is doing terrific. Which one do you want to talk about?"

The person may reply, "Well, uh, tell me about your business life." Even so, a signal has been sent that could set the stage for a future spiritual conversation.

Friends, we make split-second decisions all the time to either play it safe or tilt the conversation toward spiritual topics, and many times we shrink back. I remember a conversation I had with a retired tradesman a few years ago.

"Last week I visited a neighbor in the hospital," he said. "She lived in the same trailer park as me. She wasn't a Christian, and while I was there talking to her, I could have easily brought up spiritual matters. I mean, the door was open several times. But I played it safe. When I got home I was so angry with myself that I decided I'd go back in a couple of days and take the risk. But then I got a phone call; it turned out that she had died."

He had a look on his face as though he was in physical pain as he said to me: "Keep telling people—*when those split-second decisions come, take a deep breath, trust God, and take the spiritual road.*"

Only God knows the spiritual condition of that woman's heart at the time she died, but that man is going to wonder about it for a long time. And so I'm going to do what he asked me to do, which is to encourage you to let God guide you as you turn conversations to that which really matters.

Not that we should be overbearing or too aggressive; as we discovered earlier, evangelism is usually a process, and we need to respect that. But when the time is appropriate, when the Holy Spirit is prompting you, and when a split-second opportunity comes, follow that man's advice: "Take a deep breath, trust God, and take the spiritual road."

We can see in the Bible that Jesus did seize the opportunity to enter into a kingdom conversation with the woman at the well. And then He came to a fourth turning point. After He began talking about living water, the discussion unfolded:

> *He told her, "Go, call your husband and come back."*
> *"I have no husband," she replied.*
> *Jesus said to her, "You are right when you say you have no husband. The fact is, you have had five husbands, and the man you now have is not your husband. What you have just said is quite true."*
> *"Sir," the woman said, "I can see that you are a prophet."*[7]

It seems like up until now, the woman was intrigued by what Jesus was saying, but she may have thought He was a little odd with all His talk about living water. She may not have been taking Him very seriously.

However, Jesus came to a turning point and decided to produce evidence that would bolster His credibility. By using His divine power to look supernaturally into the circumstances of her life and then reveal them to her, He demonstrated that He was someone she would have to take seriously. And she did. She said He must be a prophet—a person sent by God, someone certainly worth listening to. The insight for us is this:

• **We should be armed with evidence to help skeptics realize that they need to be rescued.**

Just as in Biblical times, we often need to offer evidence and answer objections before a person will consider spiritual matters. In fact, before describing Jesus' encounter with the woman at the well in the fourth chapter of his Gospel, the apostle John recounts three earlier instances in which Jesus *first* produced evidence and *then* people began to believe in him.

• After meeting Jesus, Philip excitedly told his friend Nathanael that he had found the Messiah. When Nathanael expressed skepticism, Philip said, "Come and see." In other words, "You don't believe me, Nate? Go check Him out for yourself!"

As Nathanael approached Jesus to look into the matter, Jesus told him something that He only could have known through supernatural powers. Instantly, Nathanael declared: "Rabbi, you are the Son of God; you are the King of Israel."

First, Jesus offered evidence, then Nathanael believed.[8]

• The next chapter recounts how Jesus attended a wedding at Cana, where He turned 150 gallons of water into wine. The miracle provided compelling evidence of His identity, and so "his disciples put their faith in him."[9]

• While in Jerusalem at the Passover Feast, Jesus performed even more miracles. Confronted with proof of who He was, "many people . . . believed in his name."[10]

Those stories are just from John's first two chapters. Another illustration was when the imprisoned John the Baptist sent his followers to find out if Jesus really was the Messiah. Jesus told them, "Go back and report to John what you hear and see: The blind receive sight, the lame walk, those who have leprosy are cured, the deaf hear, the dead are raised, and the good news is preached to the poor."[11]

In effect, Jesus was saying: "Give John your firsthand report of the evidence that you've seen, and then he'll have no doubt."

Because of who He was, Jesus could offer supernatural proof of His identity. However, all of us can provide skeptics with evidence that demonstrates Jesus' identity.

I remember spending two weekends at our church presenting messages called "The Case for Christ," in which I showed videotapes of world-class experts whom I had interviewed about the evidence for the deity of Jesus.[12] Among those in attendance was an engineer who was a hard-core skeptic about Christianity.

At the conclusion of the second message, the person who had brought him asked, "Well, what do you think?"

The engineer looked at him for a moment, then said firmly: "I finally believe." That day he committed his life to Christ.

We'll talk in the next chapter about helping people get beyond the barriers that keep them from considering the claims of Christ. But we don't have to become junior Josh McDowells. Just being armed with basic training in defending the faith can dramatically boost our confidence.

It's like when I was teaching a course on First Amendment law to journalism students at a university in Chicago. My objective was to clarify for them the freedom that they had as journalists under the U.S. Constitution. You see, when a reporter is fuzzy about what he can or can't legally report, he begins to censor himself. He's afraid he'll run afoul of the libel laws, so he backs off from doing legitimate stories he really should be pursuing.

Similarly, when a Christian is uninformed about how much evidence supports Christianity, he often backs off from opportunities to share his faith. He squelches his evangelistic activities because he's afraid of being asked a tough question he can't answer.

When we equip ourselves with the facts, we become bolder and more willing to try to rescue spiritually imperiled people. Maybe that's why the apostle Peter, who himself argued forcefully for the faith, penned this command to all Christians: "Always be prepared to give an answer to everyone who asks you to give the reason for the hope that you have."[13]

Although we can't argue people into God's kingdom, we can help them process the Gospel by responding to their questions and providing reasons that Christianity is rational and real. In effect, we answer their questions so that they become more receptive to dealing with the ultimate question that Jesus is asking them: "Who do you say that I am?"[14]

Why not commit yourself to doing some homework about the factual foundation of your faith? Exactly why do you believe what you believe? Christian bookstores are full of resources to help you.[15] As you talk to Unchurched Harrys and Marys, you'll probably find the same basic questions coming up again and again. Among the ones I often get are:

• What about people who've never heard of Jesus? Are they going to hell?

• Why do Christians believe Jesus is the only way to heaven? Isn't it bigoted to say that only Christians know the truth? Aren't all faiths equally valid?

• Why does God allow innocent people to suffer? Why does He tolerate so much evil in the world?

• If God is all-loving, why does He send people to hell?

• I'm basically a good person. Isn't that enough?

• How do you know you can trust the Bible? Isn't it full of errors and myths?

• Aren't miracles impossible? Isn't it unscientific to believe that Jesus could perform miraculous feats?

• Doesn't science contradict the biblical account of Creation?

In fact, if you look at the top questions that evangelist Paul Little was asked during his ministry more than twenty-five years ago, they're pretty similar.[16] So if you do enough reading to be comfortable in providing reasonable responses to these issues, the end result will be that your confidence will increase.

The final turning point from the scene with the woman at the well comes after Jesus has backed up His assertion that He's the Messiah. The fifth turning point is her response:

> *Then, leaving her water jar, the woman went back to the town and said to the people, "Come, see a man who told me everything I ever did. Could this be the Christ?" They came out of the town and made their way toward him.*[17]

The Samaritan woman makes a decision so quickly that she leaves behind the waterpot she had trudged all the way to the well to fill. She rushes into town to invite people to come hear Jesus for themselves. And many flocked to Him.

Interestingly, when the disciples went into town, they only came back with some bread and dried fish. But when this woman goes into town, fresh from a spiritually supercharged encounter with Jesus, she brings back a crowd of spiritually lost people. Maybe that's because she was motivated by the importance of the situation. There's an insight for us there:

• **Those who have been rescued should understand the urgency in reaching out to rescue others.**

Remember when you were knocked to your knees by God's "amazing grace"? Someone has observed that as time goes by and the freshness wears off, sometimes it starts to become "fascinating grace," then just "interesting grace," then merely "grace," and we lose our urgency for reaching our unchurched friends. One survey showed that within the previous six months, barely one-third of Christians invited an unchurched person to attend church with them.[18]

When I sense that my fever for evangelism is starting to subside, I take some time to review in depth what my life was like before I met Jesus. Though I was undeserving, He rescued me from a life of irrelevancy and an eternity of despair.

When I think about that, my gratitude begins welling up inside of me, and I say to myself, "I know people who have *got* to experience that! They've just got to! And time's running out." Having that kind of grace-consciousness pumps me up for reaching out to the Unchurched Harrys and Marys in my life.

And one way to reach out is to do what the Samaritan woman did: invite them to a place where they can hear the Gospel. In a way, this woman partnered with Jesus, as if she had said: "Look, Jesus, would you please stay here while I run into town? I don't really know how to explain all of this to my friends, so I'll tell them all to come see you. Is that okay? Then you can tell them what you told me—all that stuff about the living water. Would you do that? Please, it's important that they understand."

Not just new believers, but *most* Christians need someone they can partner with in helping to reach their unchurched friends. But as the last chapter said, some churches are more of a hindrance than a help in evangelism. I hate to say that, but it's true.

That doesn't mean every church should stage full-fledged services for seekers each weekend, like Willow Creek and about 200 other U.S. churches do. Some churches have their traditional services on the weekend, but also offer one seeker-oriented service on Saturday night or late Sunday morning.

Others schedule periodic services or concerts that are targeted to unbelievers, perhaps monthly. I know of one church that has an outreach service called "First Sunday" on the first weekend of each month.

Some have services that are designed for worship but are "seeker friendly," which means that Unchurched Harry and Mary would feel comfortable in attending, even though the service isn't geared specifically for them.

Others stage occasional breakfasts or dinners, at which the church will have special music and a speaker who will describe his or her journey to Christ. Often the event is targeted to specific groups within the church—working women, fathers, mothers, singles, business people, or teachers, for example. What's critically important, though, is that whatever is offered speaks a language that unchurched people understand.

I remember being asked to speak at a church's Valentine's Day dinner. The organizers assured me that their members invited their unchurched neighbors to the get-together every year. But what Leslie and I encountered was extremely frustrating.

Apparently the event had degenerated over time into being merely a social gathering for Christians. As I mingled beforehand, I realized that only a handful out of the hundred people in attendance was really unchurched. On top of that, the music turned out to be the singing of hymns with lyrics like, "He hideth my soul in the cleft of a rock." Now, that's a biblical sentiment, but an unchurched person wouldn't have a clue what that was about, and even if he did, it wouldn't be true for him.

In fact, halfway through one hymn, the song leader said: "Now, you all know the words to these songs, so don't be looking at your song sheets. If I see anyone looking at the words, I'll make him sing a solo!"

I couldn't believe it! *I* didn't know the words and was positive unchurched people wouldn't either—and they were supposed to be the reason for this dinner! By the time I got up to speak, I wanted to offer an apology to the few seekers who were there.

What was truly amazing was that there was one man who did commit his life to Christ that night. And yet as Leslie and I drove home, I had to wonder how many more might have responded if these Christians had brought more unbelievers—and then not alienated them through such an inappropriate program.

By contrast, I had spoken earlier at an outreach breakfast attended by Christians who had taken seriously their responsibility to fast and pray for the non-Christians they were inviting—and then they actually brought them!

There were only about a dozen Christian businessmen who came, and each one brought one unchurched friend. The program was simple and relevant to Unchurched Harry, and for my part I merely told the story of my spiritual journey. But by the end of the morning, eight of those twelve unchurched men prayed to receive Christ. It was like a mini-revival had broken out!

The organizers didn't blow the opportunity by doing things that would turn off the very people they were hoping to reach, and God used that little breakfast in a powerful way.

Ultimately, though, we always have to keep in mind the bottom-line lesson from this scene of Jesus at the Samaritan well. It's found in these three verses:

• *Do you not say, "Four months more and then the harvest?" I tell you, open your eyes and look at the fields! They are ripe for harvest.*[19]

• *Many of the Samaritans from that town believed in him because of the woman's testimony.*[20]

• *And because of his words, many more became believers.*[21]

I could sum up the last insight from the story this way:

• **Kingdom heroes don't get bogged down in the process of evangelism; rather, they keep their eyes focused on the purpose of evangelism.**

I remember an incident involving my son, Kyle, who played on a park district soccer team when he was nine years old. Although the members of his squad were pretty good, they were losing most of their games. Finally, I said to him, "Kyle, what's the goal of soccer? What are you trying to accomplish out there?"

He thought for a moment. "Well, the coach said we're supposed to control the ball."

"That's the problem," I said. "*The goal is to put the ball in the opponent's net*. You do *that* by controlling the ball, but if you lose sight of your ultimate objective, you won't score many goals."

We all know that the process is important in evangelism. Making contact with unbelievers is necessary, building relationships with them is critical, turning conversations to spiritual matters is essential, and responding to questions is crucial.

But even though all of that is true, what ultimately matters is the end product: being used by God to rescue Unchurched Harry or Mary from spiritual Death Row. That's how we put the ball in the net. And the reality of that can fade unless we make an effort to keep focused on it.

I've lost that focus from time to time. I remember talking to a man about Christ a few years ago, and at the end of our conversation, I asked, "What can I do to help you on your spiritual journey?"

He thought for a moment, then said, "You can say a prayer for me sometime, I suppose."

I was about to stop there. I figured that later I would take the time to pray that the Holy Spirit would continue to work on him. But because of the man's hesitation before he answered, I sensed the door might still be open, and so I made a split-second decision to press a little further.

"Let me ask this," I said. "Is there a specific question or concern that's standing between you and God? If there is, I'll be glad to help you get an answer or work through it with you, because I really want to help."

Again, he paused. "Well, I guess there really isn't," he said.

So I asked, "Then is anything stopping you from receiving Christ's forgiveness and leadership right now?" Suddenly he broke into sobs. "Nothing," he said. "That's what I really want to do." So we prayed together right on the spot. He was ready that day to turn away from his sin and receive God's grace—and I had almost walked away from him.

After that happened, I thought to myself, *I never want to get so caught up in the process of evangelism that I forget the bottom line is to put the ball in the net.* In other words, to let God use me to bring people into His family.

When we keep that goal in the forefront of our minds and we live in daily anticipation that God is going to work through us, then we're ready to act when those ultimate turning points come.

In all of life, there's nothing like the adventure of evangelism. Christ Himself made that clear. In fact, to close out our scene at the Samaritan well, let's see what happened when the disciples finally returned and offered some lunch to Jesus.

But he said to them, "I have food to eat that you know nothing about."

Then his disciples said to each other, "Could someone have brought him food?"

"My food," said Jesus, "is to do the will of him who sent me and to finish his work."[22]

In other words, Jesus was telling the disciples, "You're talking about *food?* Mere physical food? While you guys were thinking about your stomachs, I was enjoying a spiritual feast that satisfied my very soul! I was nourished on the deepest of levels. I talked to a woman who was spiritually thirsty, and I explained to her about the living water that she really needs. Hey, food is okay—there's nothing wrong with eating, but no meal can compare to the taste of leading a person into God's kingdom."

Isn't that the truth? Recently a businessman excitedly described to me how he had prayed with one of his colleagues to receive Christ. "Can you believe it?" he said with a catch in his voice. "Can you believe God used someone like me to do something that important?"

He found out what it feels like to become a kingdom hero, and he'll never be the same. And when you find out, neither will you.

7

SPIRITUAL STICKING POINTS

Once I was having lunch with a well-known atheist, and I decided to ask him point-blank: "Why don't you believe in God?" He replied, "Because I don't believe in superstition."

"Hey, that's great!" I said. "Neither do I. We have something in common!"

I tried to explain to him that the dictionary defines superstition as a belief that's held in spite of evidence to the contrary. But Christianity isn't like that. It's a faith that's consistent with historical evidence.

"Superstition!" he exclaimed with a wave of his hand. "I still say it's just a silly superstition."

He was at a spiritual sticking point. As I've talked to people through the years about their spiritual journeys, often I've found they've reached an impasse that's blocking their path. In this man's case, it was his stubborn refusal, for whatever reason, to even consider the evidence for Christianity.

For others, the nature of their sticking point varies, yet the end result is the same: They're stalled in their progress toward a spiritual breakthrough. When I talk to Unchurched Harrys and Marys, I try to diagnose what's causing the blockage so I can recommend a way to get them back on track toward God.

What I'll do in this chapter is discuss five categories of spiritual sticking points that I commonly encounter in order to help you detect and deal with them as you talk with irreligious people.

- **Sticking Point #1: "I *can't* believe."**

That's the sentiment of people who have a specific intellectual or emotional issue that has halted their headway toward God. It's expressed by:

- The physician who says, "I can't believe the Bible because it conflicts with modern science."
- The mother of a sick child who says, "I can't believe in a God who permits my son to suffer when so many evil people seem to be successful."
- The lawyer who says, "I'm used to dealing with evidence and facts; I can't believe in something that we're asked to accept purely on faith."
- The corporate executive who says, "I prayed that my business would get through its crisis, but it's going down the tubes. I can't believe in a God who ignores my call for help."

Since I'm more of a "thinker" than a "feeler," I especially enjoy helping people get past intellectual roadblocks. Many times, their questions are very specific.

For instance, on Good Friday of 1990, a successful corporate attorney came into my office to discuss spiritual matters. He had been checking out Christianity for six months, and the question that had stymied him was: "How can I be sure that I can trust the Bible?"

That's a legitimate question, and we discussed it for about

three hours. Finally, there was a pause, and I said, "Do you have another question?"

"I guess I could go on forever asking questions about side issues," he said, "but, really, my main questions have been answered. I suppose now the issue is, 'What am I going to do with all of this?'"

He had jumped a hurdle concerning the reliability of Scripture, and now he was ready to deal with the Gospel. That day, five minutes before our Good Friday service started, we knelt together in my office and he received Christ's forgiveness and leadership of his life. Then we walked upstairs to a worship service that was focused on the very sacrifice that Jesus had made on his behalf.

I sat beside him as he poured out his worship to God and participated in the Lord's Supper for the first time. It was one of the most meaningful worship services I had ever attended because I was experiencing it through the grateful eyes of someone who had been saved by grace just moments before.

In discussing spiritual matters with Unchurched Harry and Mary, often I'll ask, "Is there a specific question or concern that's hanging you up in your spiritual journey?" That inquiry helps them focus with clarity on what's really blocking their path to God. Once they're able to articulate the question, then we can begin to find answers so they can continue onward toward Christ.

To help them picture their situation, sometimes I'll modify something Pascal once said and describe for them the three basic camps of people in the world. There is:

• Camp A, which consists of people who have found God;

• Camp B, which is composed of people who are seeking God and will find him;

• Camp C, for people who aren't seeking God.

I tell Unchurched Harry and Mary that there's no advantage to being in Camp C. Unless God does something dramatic, as He did when he transformed Saul of Tarsus into Paul the evangelist, Camp C is a dead end. It's a place that's populated by closed-minded people who refuse to seek after the truth.

So I encourage them to pull up their stakes, move to Camp B, and sincerely search for the truth about God. And, of course, we know from Scripture that anyone who's sincerely in Camp B will eventually end up in Camp A.[1]

Many times I challenge them to pray the kind of "seeker's prayer" that I said when I was still a skeptic. I suggest something along these lines: "God, I'm not sure You even exist, but if You do, I really want to know You. Please reveal Yourself to me. I sincerely want to know the truth about You. Put people in my life, put books and tapes in my path, use whatever means You want to help me discover who You are."

Then I encourage them to do some homework. For instance, if they think the Bible is full of errors, what are these errors specifically? Enumerate them so they can be checked out.

That's what Dr. Vic Olsen did. Dr. Olsen was a brilliant surgeon, and he and his wife, Joan, didn't believe in God because they thought modern science had established that the Bible is mythology. But they put Christianity to the test.

First they checked it out from a scientific perspective, reading a book by thirteen eminent members of the American Scientific Affiliation who showed that the Bible and science really aren't in conflict.[2] Then they checked it out from a legal perspective by reading a book by Irwin Linton, a Washington, D.C., attorney, who demonstrated how the Bible's credibility withstands even a lawyer's grueling cross-examination.[3]

They looked at it from an archaeological, medical, and even a detective's perspective. In other words, they let their curiosity propel them toward the truth, and they found that the Christian faith stands up even under rigorous examination by thinking people. Not only did they commit their lives to Christ, but they redirected their careers, using their medical skills to serve the needy in poverty-stricken Bangladesh.

Olsen wrote a book called *The Agnostic Who Dared to*

Search,[4] and that's what I challenge Unchurched Harrys and Marys to do: to take the risk of discovering the truth about God.

In law, when there's some evidence that suggests something may be true—or, in legal terminology, when there's "probable cause"—then a judge orders a full trial in which all the evidence can be thoroughly considered. What I tell skeptics is that there's clearly some evidence supporting Christianity, and therefore a full-blown examination of the facts is certainly warranted.

Given the power of Scripture, I always encourage Unchurched Harry and Mary to begin reading the Bible for themselves. Usually, it's the first time they've ever seriously looked at it. If the person is a nuts-and-bolts kind of individual, I'll suggest the gospel of Luke. Being a physician, Luke writes with the kind of straightforward clarity and detail that appeals to lawyers, doctors, scientists, and engineers.

If the individual is more artistic or philosophical, I suggest the gospel of John. If the person has a Jewish background, I prescribe the gospel of Matthew, since he emphasized the fulfillment of Old Testament prophecies in Christ.

Matthew was persuasive for Dr. Alexander Zaichenko, a prominent economist in what was then the Soviet Union. He was an atheist from a family of atheists living in a country that was officially atheistic, but in 1979 he began to ask the kind of questions that many people ask themselves as they get older: "What's life really all about? Is this all there is?"

As he groped for answers, he obtained a black-market Bible and began reading it with an open mind. He started at the beginning of Matthew, and do you know what surprised him? How boring it was!

After reading the genealogy of Jesus—"Abraham was the father of Isaac, Isaac the father of Jacob, Jacob the father of Judah and his brothers," and so forth—he began to think, "Maybe atheists are right. Maybe there's nothing to this stuff."

But he kept reading. Finally he hit the fifth chapter of

Matthew, where Jesus delivers the Sermon on the Mount, the most beautiful, provocative, profound, and challenging talk ever given on the topic of how to live.

I love the response of Dr. Zaichenko, this towering intellect who has studied all the classics, all the philosophers, all the great thinkers. "It took my breath away," he said. Instantly, he knew these weren't the words of a mere man, and he ended up committing his life to Christ.[5]

Stories like that can inspire Unchurched Harry and Mary. In addition, I try to encourage them by telling them that God isn't playing peek-a-boo with them. I point out that the very fact that they are able to seek Him is because God has enabled them to do so. Even as they search for Christ, He's reaching out to them.

Jesus said it's His mission to "to seek and to save what was lost."[6] And we know that the Lord is "not wanting anyone to perish, but everyone to come to repentance."[7]

I remember talking to an Unchurched Harry over lunch shortly before Christmas. "Nice story," he said about the biblical account of Jesus' birth, "but it's only a story."

I said, "Do you remember the part of the story where the angels told the shepherds that Jesus had been born?"

"Sure, I heard that in Sunday school," he said.

"Well, do you know what the shepherds did? They heard the news, but they didn't stop there. They went to check it out for themselves. They went to see the Messiah with their own eyes. Would you be willing to do the same thing—to check it out for yourself?"

He agreed to move from Camp C to Camp B, and I have confidence that someday he'll join me in Camp A.

So some people say, "I can't believe" based on intellectual issues, and we should encourage them to pursue the truth about God with sincerity and honesty. But others say "I can't believe" because there's some kind of an emotional barrier between them and God.

Often when I'm talking to someone who seems hung up about God, I ask about his family life and his relationship with his father, since a person's conception of his dad can greatly influence his perception of God.

In his essay, "The Psychology of Atheism," Dr. Paul C. Vitz talks about how abuse, rejection, disappointment, or abandonment by a father, or a dad's absence, can form a psychological barrier to believing in God.

He traces the problems that many noted atheists had with their dads. For instance, Sigmund Freud and Karl Marx made it clear that they didn't respect their fathers. French rationalist Baron d'Holbach was orphaned at thirteen; Bertrand Russell and Nietzsche both lost their fathers at age four; John Paul Sartre's father died before he was born; and Camus was an infant when his dad died.[8]

The son of Madalyn Murray O'Hair, the woman who founded American Atheists, Inc., chillingly described the bitter and sometimes violent relationship she had with her father. William J. Murray said that he once saw his mother trying to kill her father with a butcher knife, vowing, "I'll see you dead. I'll get you yet. I'll walk on your grave!"[9]

Murray, now a Christian businessman and evangelist, said: "It is my opinion that my mother's maniacal campaign to remove all reference to God in public schools and government, plus her heated atheistic campaigns over the years, stem back to this issue. Madalyn Murray was mad at men, and she was mad at God, who is male. Rather than confront her conscience, she determined to deny God's existence and refused to accept any moral constraints. She had to destroy all reference to God, because if there were a Deity, then He could make demands on her life."[10]

Few people go to the extreme of becoming atheists. However, a person's relationship with his father might still stymie his spiritual development. For instance, being reared in a home in which the father frequently spewed anger can prompt some people to think their Heavenly Father is similarly vengeful, and so they shy away from wanting to relate to Him.

If their dad abandoned them as a child, either emotionally or physically, they may resist a relationship with God out of fear that God will end up hurting them by abandoning them, too. They may have a shattered self-esteem, thinking their father had good grounds for leaving them because they have no intrinsic value. Consequently, they can't fathom a God who offers to love them as they are.

And there are some people who grew up in homes where they only received affirmation if they accomplished something. They may grow up feeling that they must earn everyone's love, including God's. They can get so caught up in a treadmill of trying to make themselves worthy of God that they make no headway in understanding that God's love is unconditional.

While none of these unchurched individuals would classify themselves as atheists, the bottom line is that they stop short of entering into a relationship with God.

Another emotional roadblock can be the fear of intimacy. Being an authentic follower of Jesus Christ means having a close, honest, vulnerable, dependent, and transparent relationship with Him and increasingly with His other followers—and that scares off some people. In fact, often they are people you wouldn't expect to be intimidated by the idea of relating closely to others.

"Some of the people most threatened by intimacy are warm and gregarious at a superficial level," writes John Guest. "They can chat and laugh and be very embracing in their personality style, but you never get close to them and they don't want you to. So we're not talking about a frigid personality style. We are talking about a wide range of personality styles that are mere facades behind which folks choose to live, sometimes in utter aloneness."[11]

Guest said that some of these people enter the New Age Movement because then they can search for the god they think is inside of themselves instead of searching for the true God who wants to relate to them on a personal level. They chant a meaningless mantra over and over because it's easier on them emotionally than praying painfully honest prayers to a personal God.

"The focus of such a religion is withdrawal, not engagement; self-searching, not God-searching; getting into oneself, not adoration of God," Guest said.[12]

Unchurched Harry and Mary may not realize that a fear of intimacy is really what's driving the half-hearted objections they're making to Christianity. But here's a tip-off: if you notice they tend to have an arm's-length attitude toward people, if they seem to have a superficial marriage, if they have a surface-level relationship with their children, and if they've got lots of acquaintances but no deep friendships, then those are clues that their real sticking point may be a fear of intimacy with God.

Another sign to watch for is if the person is consumed by pursuing some of the substitutes that our society offers for true intimacy, such as pornography or promiscuity. Even drinking can be a clue, since there are individuals who are dependent on alcohol to lubricate their interaction with others.

Suspecting an emotional or neurotic sticking point is one thing; doing something about it is sometimes best left to experts. When I sense this kind of issue is impeding a person's quest for God, I try to gently help him understand that he should visit a Christian counselor who can help him deal with the root cause. But I maintain my relationship with him as well, letting him know that I'm his friend regardless of circumstances.

• Sticking Point #2: "I don't *want* to believe."

Actually, few people come right out and admit they don't want to believe in the God of the Bible; it's usually more of an attitude that they try to obscure behind a smoke screen.

I suspected this was the case with a young Hindu farmer whom I met in a rural village in South India. With the help of a friend who spoke Telugu, I talked to him about the Gospel, and he began asking me several questions. When I responded to those, he started to raise some objections that were clearly half-hearted. Finally I realized that he must have some subterranean reason to keep Christ at a distance.

"Let me ask this," I said. "Is there something in your life that you're afraid you'll have to give up if you become a follower of Jesus?"

He hemmed and hawed for a while, and eventually conceded that he was involved in cockfighting, and he figured he would have to forfeit this bloody and illegal sport if he became a Christian. At last, the smoke screen had dissipated, and his real reason for resisting God came into the clear.

Of course, Americans play the game, too. I was at a Christmas party at my sister's house a few years ago when I got into a discussion about religion with a businessman who said that he thought the idea of God was irrational.

So I said, "You know, that's interesting, because that's exactly how I used to feel. May I tell you about the evidence that convinced me that it's rational to become a Christian?"

He said, "No way. That's evidence for you, not for me."

I said, "Well, evidence is evidence."

And he said, "Look, I'm not interested in hearing anything about evidence, because I don't believe it's possible to have any real evidence that there's a God." With that, he firmly closed the subject.

Now, my first thought was that he had an intellectual sticking point, that he was stymied because he didn't understand the nature of evidence. But as we chatted about several other subjects, I started to suspect that his real sticking point wasn't an intellectual one; it was a moral one.

It sounded as though he was involved in some sexual and ethical matters that he knew were contrary to the teachings of Christ, so his objection to evidence apparently was just a diversionary tactic to hide his real concern, which is that becoming a Christian would mean a radical life-change that he wasn't interested in.

Cliffe Knechtle tells the story of his conversation with a student at State University of New York who claimed the Bible was packed with mythology, though he admitted he had never read it. Knechtle challenged him to read both the book of Isaiah, which contains prophecies concerning Christ, and Matthew, which records the fulfillment of those predictions.

"I thought I would never see him again," Knechtle writes, "but the next day he approached me and said, 'I read Isaiah and Matthew. It was interesting literature. I think it speaks the truth.'"

"That's great! Are you ready to trust Christ for eternal life?"

"He said, 'No way. I have a very active sex life. I know Christ would want to change that. I don't want anyone to change that.'"[13]

At least the student was honest about why he was steering clear of God. While most people won't admit what's behind their refusal to believe, some are up front about it. For instance, Aldous Huxley, the famous author and atheist, wrote:

"I had motives for not wanting the world to have a meaning; consequently assumed that it had none, and was able without any difficulty to find satisfying reasons for this assumption. . . . For myself, as, no doubt, for most of my contemporaries, the philosophy of meaninglessness was essentially an instrument of liberation. The liberation we desired was simultaneously liberation from a certain political and economic system and liberation from a certain system of morality. *We objected to the morality because it interfered with our sexual freedom.*"[14] (Emphasis added.)

In other words, he was choosing not to believe in God so that he could continue pursuing a certain sexual lifestyle.

What I'd say to Huxley and others who raise these smoke screens is that they miss the point: that God is the God of *real* liberation. By reading the Bible, they'd see that God's goal isn't to be a curmudgeon who cramps our style, but He wants to maximize our potential and protect us from self-destructive behavior. It was God who created us in the first place; certainly He wants to see us flourish and become all that He intended us to be.

When people are hiding behind a smoke screen, sometimes it's because they see a downside to Christianity that they want to avoid, while at the same time they're overlooking Christianity's upside. So usually I'll challenge them by saying: "Why don't you do a cost/benefit analysis? That's a modern way to make a decision, isn't it? Take out some paper, divide it down the middle, and compare the benefits and costs of how you're living now with the benefits and costs of following Christ."

Think about what's on Christ's side of the ledger—He offers forgiveness, adventure, a clean conscience, security, guidance, fulfillment, relationships, comfort, peace of mind, release from guilt, the promise of eternity, power over self-destructive drives, and the unique hope that comes from being connected with the God of the universe.

Then I encourage them to play out the trajectory of their current lifestyle to its logical conclusion. "Where do you end up? How will you cope with the tragedies you're going to encounter along the way? How will you feel about yourself? And what will you draw hope from in the end?"

I tell them about my own experience. "Ever since I said to God, 'Take my life,' I've been on a white-knuckle adventure that blows the doors off of how I used to get my kicks. But go ahead," I say, "play it out for yourself."

This kind of a challenge can be useful in getting them past their diversionary tactics and to start them considering the benefits of a life—and eternity—with Christ.

• Sticking Point #3: "I don't know *what* to believe."

They hear all kinds of interpretations of the Bible. They see bickering between different denominations. They hear about doctrinal battles within denominations. They encounter some people who take the Bible literally and some who say it's just a general guideline. They hear people using the Bible to support completely contradictory and even absurd positions. They try reading the Bible and get bogged down in Leviticus.

So they throw up their hands and say, "I don't know what to believe. It seems like the meaning of the Bible changes according to who interprets it. So what's right?"

I've met people whose journey toward Christ has been derailed because they're not sure whom to believe. Between their theologically liberal friends and the fundamentalists they see on TV, they don't know who has the right answers. How can different groups of Christians read the same Bible and come up with different interpretations? Who can be trusted not to read things into the text?

One way to help these people is to explain that the key to accurately understanding the Bible is the same as the key to understanding any other communication—it's to determine what the writer meant. It's not to interpret Scripture to say what we want it to say or to read our biases into it but to figure out what the Spirit-inspired author was trying to get across in the first place.

Sometimes I use this example: I pretend that my daughter, Alison, and her boyfriend are going out for a Coke on a school night, and I say to her: "You must be home before eleven." How would you interpret that? It's pretty straightforward, isn't it?

This would never happen, but suppose it gets to be 10:45 and the two of them are still having a great time over at Portillo's Hot Dog Stand. They aren't really anxious to end the evening, so suddenly they begin to have difficulty interpreting my instructions.

They say, "What did he really mean when he said, '*You* must be home before eleven'? Did he literally mean us, or was he talking about *you* in a general sense, like people in general? Was he saying, in effect, 'As a general rule, people must be home

115

before eleven'? Or was he just making the observation that, 'Generally, people are in their homes before eleven'? I mean, he wasn't very clear, was he?

"And what did he mean by, 'You *must* be home before eleven'? Would a loving father be so adamant and inflexible? He probably means it as a suggestion. I know he loves me, so isn't it implicit that he wants me to have a good time? And if I am having fun, then he wouldn't want me to end the evening so soon.

"And what did he mean by, 'You must be *home* before eleven'? He didn't specify *whose* home. It could be anybody's home. Maybe he meant it figuratively. Remember the old saying, 'Home is where the heart is'? My heart is here at Portillo's, so doesn't that mean I'm already home?

"And what did he really mean when he said, 'You must be home before *eleven*'? Did he mean that in an exact, literal sense? Besides, he never specified 11:00 P.M. or 11:00 A.M. And he wasn't really clear on whether he was talking about Central Standard Time or Pacific Time. I mean, it's still only quarter to seven in Honolulu. And as a matter of fact, when you think about it, it's *always* before eleven. Whatever time it is, it's always before the next eleven. So with all of these ambiguities, we can't really be sure what he meant at all. If he can't make himself clear, we certainly can't be held responsible."

You see, our motives can radically color the way we interpret words. People do that with the Bible to get around teachings they don't agree with or don't want to face up to. But the way to read the Bible is to ask, "What did the communicator intend for me to understand?"

I'll concede there are difficult sections of Scripture, and well-intentioned people can legitimately debate a lot of the finer points. But when it comes to the critical message of what every person needs to know to be absolved of his past and assured of his future, there's no ambiguity.

In fact, my colleague Judson Poling telescoped the central

message of the entire sixty-six books of the Bible down to a three-second sound bite: "God made us, we blew it, Christ paid for it, we must receive Him." It's not a vague or complicated message, is it?

We have some men who come to our church from a place called Little City, which is a residential training home for people with developmental disabilities. From time to time, I used to wonder, "How much do they really understand of what goes on? How much of the message gets through? Is it too complicated for them to process?"

Then after a church service one of the men, whose name is Jack, came up to say hello. I saw that his right arm was in a cast and sling. Pointing to the injury, I said, "Did that hurt?"

Jack glanced at his arm, then said in a halting voice: "I come here . . . and hear about Jesus . . . and I think about all the pain . . . He went through for me . . . and I think . . . *'This was nothing.'*"

"Jack," I said as I hugged him, "that was the most profound thing anyone has said to me for a long time."

He understands the message.

So I tell people who are confused about what to believe that the Bible's central message is clear, pure, and unambiguous for those who aren't intent on blurring the truth for their own purposes.

The Bible summarizes it in one simple, declarative, God-inspired sentence: "Everyone who calls on the name of the Lord will be saved."[15]

• Sticking Point #4: I *do* believe; isn't that enough?"

Sometimes I'll talk to a person who grew up in a Christian home, mastered the lingo at an early age, knew the right answers in Sunday school, but has spent his life pursuing "church-ianity" instead of Christianity.

Or I'll meet a person who says he believes that Jesus is the Son of God—after all, 91% of Americans think that's true[16]—

but he'll complain that this knowledge has failed to change his life.

For some, the answer can be found in the longest distance in the world—the distance between our head and our heart. They may agree with the Gospel, but have never really appropriated it for themselves.

That was the case with a thirty-one-year-old mother of two who I met in Michigan. After attending two services at which Mark Mittelberg and I presented the Gospel and responded to questions, she came up to me and said: "I've just realized I've been playing religion all my life. I'm active at church, I'm on committees, I've heard about the Crucifixion so much since I was a child that I've been numb to it. And I realized today that I don't have a relationship with Christ. Lee, I don't want to play church anymore! I don't want to play any more games."

Though she had been immersed in church culture for years, she had never personally received Christ's forgiveness and leadership of her life—until that day.

We need to clarify for Unchurched Harry and Mary that intellectually believing in Christ is only part of the answer. One way is to use a Bible verse that provides a "spiritual equation" that spells out with math-like efficiency what it really means to become a Christian.

As I recite John 1:12, I ask them to listen for the active verbs: "Yet to all who *received* him, to those who *believed* in his name, he gave the right to *become* children of God."[17]

Those verbs make up the equation: Believe + Receive = Become.

To *believe* is to intellectually agree that Christ sacrificed Himself to pay for the wrongs we've committed. That's important, I tell them, but don't stop there. Some people sit in churches for years, stuck at this point, and they wonder why their spiritual life is stagnant.

The next verb in the equation is critically important, too. We need to *receive* God's free offer of forgiveness and eternal life.

We have to claim it for our own, because until we do that, it's not ours; it's just something we know about in our head. So it's necessary for us to admit our wrongdoing, turn away from it, and humbly accept Christ's payment on our behalf.

And then the third verb is *become*—that's the life-change that God works in us *after* we believe in Him and receive Him as our forgiver, leader, and friend. That's the transformation the apostle Paul described when he wrote: "Therefore, if anyone is in Christ, he is a new creation; the old has gone, the new has come!"[18]

The problem arises when people mistakenly get the equation inside out. They think it's "believe + become = receive."

Sure, they believe in Christ, but they feel that they need to clean up their life and make themselves acceptable before they can really receive Him. They think that if they don't get their act together first, they're going to let Christ down because they won't be able to live up to His standards. This sticking point stunts their spiritual progress.

But Jesus would say, "Look—first, believe in Me, then receive Me, and when you do that, *then* I can help you become My follower by transforming your life in ways that you could never accomplish on your own. I will empower you to change. But I can't change your life until you turn it over to Me first."

That makes sense, doesn't it? Jesus said, "I have not come to call the righteous, but sinners."[19]

I met a woman once who was stuck on the "believe + become = receive" plan. Her biggest hangup was that if she didn't scrub her life clean first, she would end up making a commitment to Christ but not being able to live a life that would honor Him. She believed that Jesus would then reject her.

"Your kids have let you down from time to time, haven't they?" I asked her.

"Sure," she said.

"When that happens, are you sorry they're your children? Do you disown them?"

"Certainly not," she replied.

"What do you do when they let you down and then ask you to forgive them?"

"Well, I forgive them, and then I try to help them grow up so they do better next time."

"That's God's approach, too," I said. "Let *Him* change you so you can become all that He wants you to be."

• Sticking Point #5: "I don't want to believe what *they* believe."

Back when I was a reporter, I used to walk through downtown Chicago and see sidewalk evangelists shouting into portable sound systems that distorted their message so much that you couldn't understand them even if you wanted to.

I'd think to myself, "Boy, I never want to end up like *that*." In other words, if Christianity requires a person to become a societal misfit who has no social life except church services and prayer meetings, count me out.

Unfortunately, Unchurched Harry and Mary often have inaccurate stereotypes about Christians that deter them from wanting to consider the faith for themselves. They see Christians as being boring, out of touch, and living a "plain vanilla" lifestyle that's devoid of excitement, challenge, or fun.

We need to show them the truth about authentic Christianity, which is that it's the most daring, fulfilling, and revolutionary way to live. In fact, I'm going to devote the next chapter to exploring the adventure of Christianity.

I'm hoping this will give you some ideas for getting people past this sticking point, and that it may also prompt you to ask yourself, "Am I living the kind of life that attracts or repels Unchurched Harry and Mary?"

8
THE ADVENTURE
OF CHRISTIANITY

Reading the classified section of the Sunday newspaper, I saw an advertisement for a new car that said: "Automatic transmission is a mandatory option."

I thought to myself, *Mandatory option? Hey, that's an oxymoron!*

An oxymoron is a combination of words that seem to contradict each other. Maybe you've heard of some famous examples—jumbo shrimp, military intelligence, gourmet TV dinner, ill health, closet space, freezer burn, old news, pretty ugly, and postal service.

Around Chicago, we have some oxymorons of our own. For instance, "Cubs victory" is one that you hear annually around town. "Northwestern University football" is another. Then there's "Greater Milwaukee area." I mean, what can be so great about *Milwaukee*?

Ted Kennedy once denounced what he claimed was a blatant attempt by Republicans to hide something from the public. He called it "a transparent cover-up." Republicans utter oxymorons, too. George Bush once called for a "flexible freeze." And there are other political oxymorons—how about "Young Republicans" and "congressional ethics?"

Do you know what a "hero sandwich" is? A delicatessen had a sign for one that was made with chicken, making it, of course, a "chicken hero."

I said to an acquaintance, "I'm collecting oxymorons; do you know any?"

"I sure do," he shot back. "Marital bliss!"

Oops, sorry I asked.

Several years ago, when I was a writer for the *Chicago Tribune* and a confirmed atheist (hey, shouldn't *that* be an oxymoron?), I was interviewing a former street gang leader named Ron Bronski. He had been a hard-drinking, glue-sniffing, hate-filled urban terrorist. After shooting a rival gang member in a revenge attack, Ron fled with his girlfriend and ended up in Portland, Oregon, where they tried to start life fresh.

But to say they started fresh would be an understatement. As it turned out, they became followers of Jesus Christ. Over time, Ron turned into a responsible citizen, a hard worker, a church member, and the father of a beautiful little girl named Olivia.

His conscience bothered him, however, because there was a warrant for his arrest in Chicago, and he knew that the right thing to do was to turn himself in. So after much agonizing and soul-searching, he said good-bye to family and friends, took a train to Chicago, and surrendered to police.

His lawyer tipped me to the story. I interviewed the cynical police detectives who knew Ron from his gang days, and they said they were genuinely amazed at the transformation that had taken place in his life. They were convinced that it was authentic. And then I interviewed Ron. After he told me his story about how Christ had revolutionized his outlook and attitudes, I felt compelled to ask him one last question.

"You lived a pretty wild life here in Chicago," I said. "There was a lot of action, a lot of adventure, a lot of adrenaline. Now that you've become a Christian, how are you adjusting to the quiet life of a church mouse?" Ron looked at me as if that were the craziest question he had ever heard. Then he told me, in blunt terms, that there was no adventure in the world like Christianity.

I thought to myself, *There's an oxymoron! Who would ever put "adventure" and "Christianity" into the same sentence?*

I knew what adventure was all about, and it was nothing like sitting in a church pew with folded hands while singing a hymn that somebody wrote 200 or 300 years ago.

Adventure is the exploits of space explorers, the flights of manned balloons over the Atlantic, the exploration of sunken seventeenth-century galleons in the Caribbean. Those courageous enterprises inspire others to get a taste of adventure themselves.

In fact, lots of people are going on adventure vacations these days. There are 5000 travel agents around the country who provide opportunities for tourists to go hiking in the Himalayas, rafting on a wild Colorado river, exploring in Katmandu, bicycling along the Great Wall of China, skiing a glacier in Alaska, trekking through the Andes Mountains, sailing around the Virgin Islands, visiting the Masai tribesmen in Tanzania, snorkeling with the tuna off Fiji, riding a wagon train through Wyoming, or going on a photo safari in Kenya.

The big rage isn't bobbing around on the Love Boat anymore; it's sailing to exotic ports in the tropics or Antarctica. Some people take working vacations to help scientists with research projects like mapping coral reefs off the Dutch West Indies.

Most of us will never traipse around the world on an adventure, but we envy people who do. We watch Jacques

Cousteau on television and try to imagine what it would be like to sail with him on the Calypso.

Those are adventures. But I didn't see anything particularly exciting about living the boring, rigid, black-and-white life of a Christian.

That's how a lot of Unchurched Harrys and Marys feel. They balk at considering Christianity because of an unstated fear that if they commit themselves to Christ, all of the fulfillment and adventure will be drained from their lives.

As for me, during my investigation of Christianity I was quietly dreading the possibility of becoming a Christian and having to give up my late-night bar-hopping with the boys. I just couldn't picture myself becoming a churchgoer and serving for months at a time on some stodgy committee whose sole purpose was to decide whether to buy hymnals with blue or red covers.

But in spite of these concerns, at the end of my investigation I concluded that Jesus Christ is exactly who He claimed to be. And after I gave Him my life, I made an absolutely amazing discovery—Ron Bronski had been right!

I learned that there was nothing more exciting, more challenging, and more adventure-packed than living as a devoted follower of Jesus Christ. What I found out is that there's a big difference between *thrills* and *thrills that fulfill*.

Thrills are those short-lived, shallow, self-gratifying injections of adventure that I used to pump into my life in a desperate attempt to grab for the gusto before getting snuffed out forever. These thrills are like the colorful fireworks that explode in the sky on the Fourth of July, but then quickly fade into blackened embers.

But thrills that fulfill are those thrills that come when you truly submit your life to God and you pray a dangerous prayer like, "Here I am, Lord, wholly available to You."

These are the thrills you feel when God uses you to have an impact on other human beings that will last for eternity.

They're the thrills that come when God gives you a role to

play in the biggest adventure of all time—the building of His kingdom.

It's the thrill that comes as you feel the glow of God's approval when you've been obedient to Him and when you've extended His love to people in need.

It's the thrill that comes when you pour yourself into the lives of others, and you witness how God begins to work in them, to transform them, cleanse them, relieve their guilt, and give their lives meaning and security. You're part of that!

It's the thrill you feel when you go out in faith onto a limb and say, "Lord, I'm going out further than I've ever gone before, and I'm scared. My heart's pounding and my palms are sweaty, but I know You'll protect me, so here I go."

Eugene Peterson put it this way, "The word 'Christian' means different things to different people. To one person it means a stiff, upright, inflexible way of life, colorless and unbending. To another, it means a risky, surprise-filled venture, lived tiptoe at the edge of expectation. . . . If we get our information from the biblical material, there is no doubt that the Christian life is a dancing, leaping, daring life."[1]

That's how life was meant to be lived—*at the edge of expectation*.

After becoming a Christian, I got involved with helping a ministry in South India that was providing homes for abandoned children, offering medical and dental care to the poverty-wracked residents of remote villages, and bringing the message of Christ into an oppressive and sometimes hostile spiritual environment.

I can remember standing in a tiny Indian village, surrounded by mud huts with thatched roofs and open sewage ditches, in a place where Westerners rarely go, and being used by God to bring His message of hope to these spiritually desperate people—men who worshiped snakes and women whose self-esteem had been crushed by their culture.

I especially recall one lower-caste young man, dressed in faded blue shorts and a tattered T-shirt, who had been told his whole life that he was worth nothing and that he didn't matter. But when he heard for the first time the message of God's love for him and Christ's sacrifice on his behalf, and when he understood that the God of the universe knew him by name and cared immeasurably for him, he just started sobbing. He was overwhelmed by gratitude and amazement.

I'll never forget my feelings that day. All I could do was marvel that I was on the other side of the planet from my home, in the middle of nowhere, late at night, being used by God to bring this young man the news that was going to alter his life and eternity from that day forward.

I put my arm around him, looked up at the sky, and said, "Thank You, Lord, for the adventure of following You."

But you don't have to travel all the way to Andhra Pradesh, India, to find adventure as a Christian. You can find it day by day, person by person, in your own home town. And Unchurched Harry and Mary need to understand that.

They don't need merely to be *told* that Christianity is the adventure of a lifetime; they need to see that reality played out in your life. Because if you're living a boring, lukewarm Christian life of drudgery and rule-keeping, you may be doing more damage to your friends than all the scandals involving the televangelists. You're sending a message that Christianity is "a stiff, upright, inflexible way of life, colorless and unbending," and it was certainly never intended to be that.

It's not easy to explain to an unbeliever why the adventure of Christianity is unlike any other. It reminds me of watching my television set, which has wavy lines through the picture, faded color, and periodically has to be slapped on the side to get rid of the interference. Sometimes a commercial for a new Zenith or Magnavox set will come on the screen, and the announcer will say, "Look how great the picture is!" But I can't appreciate the quality of that new set because my own TV is distorting the picture.

That's sort of what it's like for persons whose eyes have not been fully opened by Jesus Christ and yet they're trying to peer into the lives of committed Christians and understand the dynamics of faith. They have trouble appreciating the adventure of Christianity because their own jaded perceptions are distorting the picture that they see.

When I talk about the adventure of Christianity, Unchurched Harry and Mary sometimes ask what the difference is between Christianity and any other socially worthwhile cause, such as environmentalism or political issues. In other words, what makes the Christian adventure unique? I explain that there are many unique qualities of the Christian life, and then I zero in on three. The first is that when we enlist on the adventure of Christianity:

WE HAVE A COMMANDER WE CAN COUNT ON.

There's a story about an Army sergeant and a private who were doing survival training in the Rocky Mountains. As they made their way through the woods, suddenly they encountered a big, angry grizzly bear that was about to attack them.

Quickly the sergeant sat down, ripped off his heavy hiking boots, took some running shoes out of his backpack, put them on, and was lacing them up in a hurry.

The private stood there watching. "Excuse me, sir," he said. "Do you really think you're going to be able to outrun that bear?"

"Well, private, I don't have to outrun the bear," replied the sergeant. "I only have to outrun *you*."

The point is that the world offers us leaders who don't really have our best interests at heart. We've seen politicians who make all kinds of promises but then fail us in the end. Many people know what it's like to work for a boss whose sole allegiance is to himself. In other words, if the situation becomes him or you, he's going to save himself, as the sergeant was trying to do.

I know of only one sure-fire way to determine whether my leader is really in my corner: *Is he willing to take a bullet that was meant for me?* It would be like the sergeant in the story saying, "Private, you run for safety; I'll stay here and take on this bear."

Jesus said, "Greater love has no one than this, that he lay down his life for his friends."[2] And that's exactly what Jesus Himself willingly did for us—He sacrificed His life so that we might have access to eternity with God. To me, that's concrete confirmation of His genuine love for us.

What's more, we can count on Him for direction. The moment we receive Christ's forgiveness and leadership in our life, the Holy Spirit takes up residence and offers us an internal compass for our spiritual safari. With a regular compass, all you have to do is find true north and then all the other directions fall naturally into place. And once we get calibrated with the Holy Spirit, then every other facet of our life begins to fall into place.

Even beyond that, our commander offers us strength and peace—but those sound like platitudes, don't they? Don't you wish we had a laboratory where we could put those promises to the test?

A few years ago, two of my colleagues did have their faith tested. I had sent Rob Wilkins and Larry Kayser to Haiti to research a story for our church magazine about a hospital we were helping on the northern part of the island. While down in that politically volatile country, they got caught in the middle of one of Haiti's periodic revolutions.

As they hurriedly boarded a seven-seat, twin-engine airplane in a dash for safety, two rebels jumped a fence and stormed the plane. They fired a machine gun into the air to show they meant business, and they threatened to kill everyone on the plane unless they were flown away from Haiti—fast.

The plane took off. For the passengers, all of whom were Christians, it was like looking death in the face. With a gun being waved in front of him and another hijacker nervously holding a bomb, Rob said later, "I was wondering whether it would be better to get a bullet through the brain or be blown into little pieces."

Not many of us have been thrust into situations where our lives were hanging by a thread. For several tense hours, Rob and Larry discovered what that was like as the plane flew toward Miami, where ultimately the FBI captured the hijackers without anyone having been harmed.

After Rob and Larry returned home, their friends gathered for a celebration, and we asked them to describe their experience. Though we were all followers of Christ, I think we were secretly wondering, "How would my faith stand up if there were a machine gun pressed up against my chin? Do I really have a commander I can count on?"

"It was a weird experience sitting next to somebody who has your life in his hands," Rob said. "But I kept thinking, well, he doesn't *really* have my life in his hands. Those of you who know me know that I don't just say things to sound Christian, but this incident brought home the reality of death, and it's an incredible experience to see that your faith can stand up to that reality.

"That isn't to say there wasn't any anxiety. But about half an hour into the flight there came over both of us—in fact, we even talked about it on the plane—a sense of peace. The worst thing we could do is die, and for a Christian, that isn't so bad. Our faith stood up in the reality of death."

Said Larry: "I've often wondered when I've heard people who have been in situations like that and they would talk about this amazing sense of God's grace, and I wondered if I was ever in that situation what would happen. And what did happen was grace.

"There were no tears, there was no anger, there was no yelling. There was absolute peace on that airplane. One verse that came to mind at the time was 'Do not be anxious about anything.'[3] I sat there and said, 'Okay, God, Your Word says to be anxious for nothing, but I can't do that right now. If this is really Your Word, *You're* going to have to do it.' And He did."[4]

Friends, we do have a commander we can count on. Christians aren't following a cosmic General Custer into battle; we're following a God who has the big picture, who has our best interests at heart, and who has the power to help us.

Is that what we're communicating to the Unchurched Harrys and Marys in our lives? Do they see us living a life of active reliance on God, where we stretch the envelope of our faith and freshly experience God's faithfulness toward us? Have you found, firsthand, that you have a commander you can count on?

Or are you living a spiritually safe life that sends a subtle message to your unchurched friends that you're really no different from them except that you have fewer bad habits and spend an hour in church on Sundays?

The fact that we have a commander that we know we can count on distinguishes Christianity from all other adventures. And a second unique characteristic of the cause of Christ is this:

WE HAVE A MISSION THAT REALLY MATTERS.

There's the joke about a jet that was flying coast to coast in the middle of the night. Two hours into the flight, the pilot's voice came over the intercom to say:

"Ladies and gentlemen, this is your captain speaking. We're flying at an altitude of 37,000 feet and at a speed of 575 miles an hour. I'm afraid we have some good news and some bad news. The bad news is that we're lost; we have absolutely no idea where we are. But the good news is that we're making excellent time!"

That's a good analogy for my life before Christ. I was racing headlong through a journalism career, working at breakneck speed, accumulating goodies along the way, but where was I really going? What was I accomplishing that was going to make any difference in an ultimate sense?

One day when I was working at the *Tribune*, I went down the hall to the newspaper's library where clippings of articles are filed away for future reference. I needed to look at a particular article I had written about a year earlier, so the librarian took me over to a huge file cabinet.

"We take one copy of every article," she said, "and we file it away under the name of the reporter who wrote it." She pulled out a broad, shallow file drawer, and inside were rows packed with yellow envelopes that were stamped LEE STROBEL. "Here you go," she said. "These are all your articles."

I had a strange sensation as I looked inside that drawer. Here was the substance of my entire life's work at the *Tribune*. Suddenly it struck me: *This is what I'm killing myself for?* I'm trading my life for a drawer full of neatly folded newspaper clippings that are turning brittle and yellowing around the edges? At that moment, it didn't seem like a fair trade. In fact, I was getting ripped off!

Some people trade their entire life for a drawer full of shopping receipts, or for a wall full of plaques, or for notches on their bedpost, or for a collection of empty bottles. Is it really a fair trade?

Someone once said that nobody will lie on his deathbed, look back at his life, and say to himself with regret, "Darn! I wish I had spent more hours at the office! I wish I had worked harder so my commissions would have been bigger. And if I had only put a little more cash into treasury bills!" What's really important in life probably gets sorted out during our last moments on earth.

My guess is that most of us will look back and ask ourselves, "What kind of contribution did I make to the world? Did I fritter away my time or did I do something that's going to outlast me? Did I leave a mark on people that's going to fade, or did I leave a mark that's eternal? When God nudged me to take a risk, did I trust Him or play it safe? What did I do to lay up treasures for myself in heaven?"

There's a New York City resident whose name is listed in the *Guinness Book of World's Records* more than anyone else's. He's recognized fifteen times for such feats as yodeling nonstop for 27 hours, running while juggling three balls for 3 1/2 hours, and doing nonstop somersaults for more than twelve miles. He's immortalized in that book—but for what?

In contrast, Jesus gives His followers an important role in the most sweeping, daring, exciting, and meaningful enterprise of all time—His rescue of the world. He gives us an opportunity to impact our friends, neighbors, colleagues, and relatives with a message that can rewrite their life and eternity. What mission could be more fulfilling or challenging?

One problem is that sometimes we don't see our individual contribution as mattering very much. I heard a story about a man who was walking along the street and he came upon a construction site. There were three laborers, all performing the same task, but when he asked them what they were doing, their answers varied. "Breaking rocks," said the first laborer. "Earning my living," said the second. But the third said: *"I'm helping to build a cathedral."*

Christians who live a life of adventure are able to see themselves as cathedral builders, people who are part of a greater vision of building God's kingdom. While their role may seem obscure to others, they know they're making a meaningful contribution to a mighty and worthwhile enterprise.

It's like the volunteers who serve at our church by making duplicates of audio tapes containing messages given at our outreach services. They stand for hours at machines to crank out thousands of tapes, yet they don't see their task as menial or insignificant. They know that God can use those messages in powerful ways, and so they share in the adventure of God's touching human lives. That motivates them! They have a mission that really matters, as does every Christian who has an accurate perspective of his contribution to the kingdom.

Psychologist Gary Collins has studied Christians who make

a difference. He defines a difference-maker as "an individual whose attitudes, values, and actions encourage, free, equip, teach, help, or in some other way benefit the lives of others."[5] They're people who know God has given them a mission, and though it may be a behind-the-scenes role, they know it matters because they're serving where God wants them to serve. As the Bible says, "Anyone . . . who knows the good he ought to do and doesn't do it, sins."[6]

Our minds tend to race to big-name Christian leaders when we think of difference-makers. Yet we should never underestimate the impact being made in the trenches of everyday life by people who faithfully extend love to the forgotten, serve people who are hurting, and seek God's blessings for others.

Another attitude that can hold us back from becoming a difference-maker is our feeling of inadequacy. We ignore God's nudging to get into the fray of His work because we think we're incapable of making a contribution. But the amazing truth is that God sees potential in us that we don't even see in ourselves.

Think of Gideon, the farmer who was cowering in fear from the Midianite marauders who would periodically sweep through his land. Gideon thought of himself as being the least member of the weakest family in the region.[7] Even so, when an angel appeared to him, guess how he addressed Gideon?

He didn't say, "Hey, coward!" or "Hey, you with the yellow stripe down your back!" He said: "The Lord is with you, mighty warrior."[8]

God saw potential in Gideon that Gideon didn't recognize in himself. God knew that when He teamed up with Gideon, this once-fearful farmer could accomplish amazing feats that he never could have imagined.

Throughout history, God has chosen ordinary people to accomplish extraordinary goals. That way the credit goes more readily where it ought to go: back to God. Jesus' disciples weren't exactly out of the pages of *Gentleman's Quarterly*, and yet they were catapulted into reshaping the history of the world.

Collins tells the story of his own elderly mother, who doubted whether she was still capable of making any difference.

> A few years ago, her world collapsed when my father died. Because of failing eyesight she could no longer drive, so the family car was sold. Arthritis slowed her walk and kept her from venturing too far from the little apartment where she lived by herself. After a while, the previously solicitous neighbors went back to their busy lives and left her alone to cope with loneliness and widowhood. Her attitude has always been good and my mother rarely complains, but she's puzzled by one thing.

> "I don't know why I'm still here," she says. "I can't do anything. I have to depend on other people if I want to get groceries or go anywhere. My life doesn't make much of a difference to anybody. The only thing I can do is pray."

> So the lady has become a prayer warrior. Her intercessions flow continually to heaven, and many of us are confident that her prayers make a significant difference.[9]

Let's pause for a moment to ask some tough questions. Do you really see yourself as being involved in a mission that matters? Are you actively engaged in God's redemptive work—not playing church but taking a meaningful role in advancing the kingdom of God? When your unchurched acquaintances see you, do they see a person who is making a difference, either directly or indirectly, in the lives of others?

Are you cooperating with God so He can maximize your contribution to His work? If not, where are you holding back? Dealing with these issues is important because you may be the only Christian your friend knows, and what he sees in your life will give him an impression of Christianity that can either attract him or repel him.

But God doesn't just give us a mission and then dispatch us

on a spiritual adventure. He equips us first. And that's another aspect of Christianity that distinguishes it from other adventures:

WE'RE EMPOWERED BY EQUIPMENT THAT'S UNEQUALLED.

The Bible says that God instills in every believer a phenomenon called a spiritual gift—a divine enablement so that each individual can share in the adventure of furthering God's plan.[10] It may be a gift of teaching, evangelism, leadership, administration, helping, giving, mercy, hospitality, discernment, encouragement, shepherding, counseling, or something else, but every Christian is equipped so that he can have a piece of the action in building God's kingdom and serving others in His name.

My wife, Leslie, used to complain that she was the only Christian in history who hadn't received a spiritual gift. For several frustrating years, she couldn't find a niche in serving God that seemed natural and productive.

Then she went through a program designed to help people discover their giftedness, and she found out that God has given her a spiritual gift of shepherding. That's the divine ability to guide and nurture individuals or groups as they grow in their faith. Since then she has used her gift to help many women grow in their relationship with God.

I was explaining spiritual gifts to my son, Kyle, when he was younger, and it soon became clear that he wasn't quite catching the concept yet.

"Dad, I think I know your gift," he said.

"What is it?" I asked.

"You have the gift of being able to bite into ice cream without your teeth hurting."

Now, that is a real gift, but I don't think it's a *spiritual* gift. Actually, I discovered my main gift one day when I was working as assistant managing editor of a chain of suburban daily newspapers. My boss knew that I was a Christian, and at the end of a horribly hectic day during which nearly everybody had lost his or her composure, he asked me, "Strobel, how did you get through the day without blowing your top? What's this Christianity thing to you?"

Nobody had ever asked me that before. I wasn't sure what to say, but I went over to his office door, closed it, and spent the next forty-five minutes telling him as best I could about how Jesus Christ had radically redirected the trajectory of my life.

When I emerged, I felt as if my entire life had been a movie shot in very grainy black and white film with scratchy sound—yet, that forty-five minutes had been filmed in vivid technicolor and rich Dolby stereo. I discovered my gift was evangelism, the divinely assisted ability to share the Gospel with others.

There's no way I can express the fulfillment I experience when God uses me to communicate the most important message in history to a person whose eternity is hanging in the balance. Where do you find stakes higher than that? Where do you find a mission more meaningful?

If you're a follower of Jesus Christ, you've been granted a spiritual gift, too. Have you discovered, developed, and deployed it? When your unchurched friends see how God uses you to have an eternal impact on others, that speaks volumes about authentic Christianity.

I call people who aren't actively using their spiritual gift "tour-bus Christians." That's because they're driving comfortably through life as they gaze out the window at others who are elbow-deep in the daily adventure of serving God and working among spiritually needy people.

Tour-bus Christians are insulated from the real-world activity and excitement of God's work. They may avoid some of the pain that's involved, and they may protect themselves from the difficulties and struggles, but there's no real adventure on a tour bus. They miss out on the excitement of living at the edge of expectation. They don't experience the tremendous counter-cultural truth that the more a Christian pours himself out serving others in God's name, the more God will fill him to overflowing. The adventure comes when you tell the tour bus to stop, and you jump off and say:

"Lord, I want to get into the fray. I want to play a role in the biggest adventure story of all time. Use me to make a difference. Use me to impact a young person for You. Use me to solve someone's problem. Use me to soothe someone's pain. Use me to answer someone's prayer. Use me to feed someone who's hungry. Use me to rescue a child. Use me to bring someone to You. Use me to ease someone's loneliness. Use me to raise a godly family. Use me to deepen someone's faith. Use me to cheer someone on. Use me to help a broken person understand that he's precious in Your sight. Use me to touch lives in Your name.

"I don't want to just observe cathedrals through my bus window; I want to roll up my sleeves and build one! Lord, use me to build a living cathedral dedicated to your glory."

Don't you yearn to pray a prayer like that and really mean it?

Christian adventurer Tim Hansel said: "The great tragedy of today's convenient world is that you can live a trivial life and get away with it."[11] Let's be honest: "Trivial Christian life" ought to be an oxymoron!

There's a Christian cliché that says, "Your life may be the only Bible your friend ever reads." Like a lot of clichés, there's truth at its core. What does your unchurched friend see when he looks at the way you live out your faith? Does he see someone who dutifully goes to church every Sunday, but who never extends the compassion of Christ into the lives of others? Or do they see someone whose faith is "a risky, surprise-filled venture, lived tip-toe at the edge of expectation?"

Earlier in this chapter I mentioned Ron Bronski, the gang leader-turned-Christian who surrendered on an attempted murder charge for wounding a rival gang member. I wasn't a

Christian when I met him, yet I was impressed by the vibrancy and character-changing power of his faith.

I had seen hundreds of obviously guilty defendants who tried to exploit every possible loophole to avoid the punishment they deserved, but Ron readily admitted his guilt and stood prepared to accept the consequences. Ironically, it was an article by me, then an atheist, that helped persuade a judge to give him probation instead of sending him to the penitentiary.

Fifteen years later, I wanted to track down Ron so that I could thank him for having lived out a faith that helped point me toward Christ. As I used my old journalistic skills to find him, I was hoping that Ron would still have a strong relationship with God.

Finally, I located a minister at a Portland church that Ron had attended in the 1970s. But when I called to ask about him, the pastor said, "I'm sorry, but Ron doesn't go to this church anymore."

My heart sank. "Do you know if he's still following Christ?" I asked. "I really need to know."

"Oh, of course he is!" came the reply. "Ron's in the ministry now. He's the pastor of his own church in a public housing project in Portland. I'll give you his phone number."

When I finally contacted Ron, it was his turn to be amazed. "I can't believe you're a Christian," he kept saying. "The last time I saw you, you thought Christianity was a bunch of garbage."

Today, with Christ as our common denominator, Ron and I have become good friends. In fact, I'm writing these words on a Sunday afternoon, just after returning home from Chicago's tough Logan Square area. That's the same turf that Ron and his gang, the Belaires, had terrorized during the 1960s.

I went to hear Ron tell his story at Armitage Baptist Church, which is located inside a building that once housed a dance hall where he used to get into drunken brawls.

"When I was a gang leader, I thought I knew what freedom

was," he told the crowd this morning. "Let me tell you about the true freedom I've found."

For Ron Bronski, the adventure continues. And seeing his life, more and more people are being pointed toward Jesus Christ. I want the same thing to be said about my life. How about you?

9

WHEN YOU'RE MARRIED TO UNCHURCHED HARRY (OR MARY)

The call came at 3:30 P.M. on Easter. Theresa was crying.

"Holidays are always the worst," she said between sobs. "But today, he really went too far. He's been making fun of me, saying I'm weak, saying I believe ridiculous things, saying the church is just trying to get my money. I'm tired of defending myself. I don't know what to do anymore. Why won't he just let me believe what I want? Why does he have to ruin everything? It was bad enough having to go to Easter services by myself; why does he have to destroy the rest of my day, too?"

Theresa (not her real name) is a committed follower of Jesus Christ whose husband is a hard-core unbeliever, and it's slowly and painfully ripping apart the fabric of their relationship. And she's not alone. Leslie and I have encountered many Christians, men and women, whose spiritual life is being stunted and whose emotional life is in anguish because they are married to a spouse who refuses to take any interest in God.

Maybe you're in a situation like that, or perhaps you know someone who is. If so, you understand the suffering involved. You won't be surprised at this letter that a woman sent me a few weeks after I spoke at her church:

When I think of your message concerning being married to an unbeliever, I still get emotional. Being an usher at the church, I must have looked pretty silly crying through half the service, but when I completely broke down during the prayer at the end—well, maybe I should turn in my usher's badge.

Unchurched Harrys and Marys can't understand why their decision to remain "spiritually neutral" sends such damaging tremors through their marriage. But it does. Some of the most frustrated individuals I know are those whose spouse doesn't share their devotion to Christ. Every time they see a Christian couple whose marriage has a dynamic spiritual dimension, they yearn for what's missing in their own married life.

Here's the part that's often missed: *Some of the friction in these situations stems from the inability of Christian spouses to understand the emotions of their unbelieving partner.*

And many times they have difficulty processing their own feelings, too. When that's added to the tendency of Christians to go overboard in trying to win their spouse to Christ, the marriage can become increasingly turbulent.

I know; I've been through it. So has Leslie. In fact, let me tell you the story of the marital stress we endured during nearly two years of our relationship. Maybe getting inside the mind of an unchurched spouse will help you weather the storm of a spiritually imbalanced marriage.

OUR MARRIAGE WITHOUT GOD

Think back to 1966. Radio stations were playing the Beatles' new hit "Michelle." People were spending their evenings watching *Peyton Place*, *The Monkees*, and *The Dick Van Dyke Show* (no, not the reruns; the *originals*). You could buy bread for nineteen cents a loaf and a new Ford Fairlane for $1,595. Seems like a long time ago, doesn't it?

That's the year Leslie and I met—in fact, to be precise it was on December 26, 1966, that a friend of mine introduced us. We were fourteen years old, and it was love at first sight.

After all, how could Leslie resist someone as cool as I was? I was wearing a big-collar, blue-and-white polka dot shirt; a cream-colored Levi waist-length jacket; silver sharkskin pants with a four-inch belt and mammoth buckle; and big-heeled, pointed black suede boots. Hey, the clothes make the man, right? (C'mon, we *all* dressed like goofballs in the '60s!)

Leslie and I dated throughout high school, breaking up occasionally but always getting back together. A year after I went to college, Leslie moved down to Columbia, Missouri, to join me. We were married after my sophomore year.

It takes me only six words to sum up the role that God played during the early years of our marriage: *He just wasn't on our agenda*. Our lives were packed with far more pressing matters.

After I finished college, we moved to a high-rise apartment not far from Tribune Tower in downtown Chicago. Leslie was busy with her banking career, I was beginning to climb the ladder at the *Tribune*, we were starting a family, then taking a break for law school, and finally buying a house. Frankly, there was just no room for God, even if He did exist.

Even so, we had a happy marriage. Sometimes I hear Christians say that unbelievers can't really be happily married because they don't know what true love is. Well, we knew enough about it to be pretty content. We were best friends, living an exhilarating life, and for the most part didn't have any worries.

This is how I picture our life together back then: It was as if Leslie and I were driving through life in a convertible sports car. We were laughing and joking. I had one arm around her, and I was waving the other hand to people as we zoomed by. "Look at the Strobels," they'd say. "Aren't they happy? Aren't they doing great?"

You see, we didn't need to have a hand on the steering wheel because the momentum of our love kept us traveling down the highway in a straight line.

But the problem was that we were oblivious to the curves up ahead. We couldn't see the emotional curve we would encounter when my father would die. We didn't foresee the rough road we would face when we'd fall into financial difficulties. We didn't see the potholes that were coming when we would have to decide how to raise our kids—do we follow Dr. Spock or some other expert? And, finally, we weren't looking ahead to the inevitable fork at the end of the road, when one of us would eventually die, and the other would be left to cope alone with the loss.

Where would we get the strength and courage to muscle our life through those curves? Who would get us back on the right path after we'd slid off onto the shoulder? The truth is that we were oblivious to the deeper issues of life. But were we happy? Yes, we were—at least on a superficial level.

UNDERSTANDING MY MINDSET

Our happiness went into a skid in the fall of 1979. That's when Leslie told me of her choice to follow Jesus Christ, and her decision initiated the most tumultuous era of our relationship.

Christians can understand some of the emotional pain that was going on inside Leslie, but most of them can't appreciate the corrosive feelings that were eating away at me. Let me describe my emotional state to help you understand what motivates the behavior of some unchurched spouses.

First, I was feeling hurt. That might sound like an odd reaction, but all of a sudden I felt like I was less in Leslie's eyes. I thought I was losing her respect. The people she was starting to look up to and emulate were Christians who had authentic

143

relationships with Jesus Christ. She was meeting all sorts of new people through church and she seemed so impressed by their spirituality that I was feeling as if she was looking down at me. Of course, she wasn't, but that didn't stop me from feeling devalued.

If these people were to be respected because of their devotion to Christ, then what's the logical flip side of that? I felt that Leslie's respect for me would dwindle because I wasn't committed to God.

And I wondered what would happen if she insisted on raising our children as Christians. Would they think less of me, too? I was concerned that they'd grow up pitying poor old Dad because, after all, he's just a pagan on the road to hell. I didn't want my kids feeling sorry for me. I wanted them to respect their dad, and maybe that wouldn't be possible if they saw me falling short in an area that they had been taught was important.

I remember one Sunday morning Leslie was getting dressed to go to church while I was still in bed. She said to me in a very pleasant tone of voice, "Do you want to come with me?"

The truth was that going to church was the last thing on my mind. What I wanted to do was to roll over and try to sleep off my hangover. But I'll tell you something: I felt like I was losing her. I felt like she was being pulled away from me and into a new sphere of relationships where I didn't feel comfortable.

So I snapped, "Yeah, okay, I'll go." I stomped around the house, slammed some doors, refused her offer to fix me breakfast, and got dressed. It was raining as we left the house, and we got wet as we tried to get into the car. I was in an ornery mood, driving much too fast on the slick roads, even hydroplaning as I plowed through some big puddles. Every once in a while I'd swear at the weather.

Finally, Leslie broke down in tears. "Look, I'm not twisting your arm," she said. "If you don't want to go, don't. Just let me go in peace."

I had just made matters worse. I felt obligated to go to

church because I thought I was losing her, and yet I ended up pushing her further and further away from me.

Another emotion I felt was frustration. I was frustrated because, for the first time in our relationship, our values were at odds. For instance, we had always been in agreement on how to spend our money. We were pretty loose with our finances, dipping into debt to indulge ourselves whenever we felt we deserved it. But now Leslie wanted to give money to the church, and I blew my top. Money was very important to me, and I felt that she was going to waste it by giving it to a bunch of charlatans.

Leslie felt so strongly about giving to the church that she got a part-time job just so she could contribute more to help the ministry expand. I couldn't relate to that. It grated on me because I thought of all the fun ways we could spend that extra cash, and yet, at least to my way of thinking, it was going down the drain.

And I felt afraid, too. I feared that Leslie was going to turn into a wild-eyed religious fanatic—you know, some sexually repressed prude who would put a damper on all of our fun.

Was she going to embarrass me in front of my friends? Was she going to shame me every time I drank too much? Was she going to spill details about our private life in her prayer group? Was she going to reject all of our old friends? Were her church buddies going to poke fun at me behind my back? Was she getting hooked up with a cult that was going to control every aspect of her private life?

To me, it was a clear-cut case of bait and switch. I married one Leslie, and now she was changing into something I hadn't bargained for. That didn't seem fair. Though I liked the new Leslie, I wanted the old Leslie back!

Finally, I was experiencing anger. I'm talking about *serious* anger. If you had asked me back then why I was so mad, I probably couldn't have told you. I just knew that I was infuriated much of the time.

Now, as I look back, I can pinpoint the root of my rage.

Basically, as Leslie pursued a godly lifestyle more and more, her behavior increasingly accentuated the difference between that lifestyle and my own.

In other words, the more she sought after purity, integrity, honesty, tolerance, and forgiveness, the more obvious it became that my own life and relationships were corroded with cynicism, bitterness, superficiality, and self-centeredness. It was as if Leslie were unwittingly holding up a mirror and I was seeing myself for how I really was, and I didn't like the picture.

The Bible calls it being convicted of sin, and it made me angry because I didn't want to face it. I would much rather maintain the illusion that I was a wonderful guy and that everything in my life was great.

All of these emotions boiled inside of me like liquid in a cauldron. Disagreements broke out. Arguments erupted. I'd stomp out of the house instead of trying to work things out. I couldn't diagnose what was going on, but I knew our marriage was headed downhill—fast.

If you're married to a non-Christian, it's important to understand the feelings that may be haunting him. And it's important to know that some of his emotions, as difficult as they are to endure, can actually be a healthy part of the process of coming to God.

For instance, the anger that stemmed from my feeling convicted of sin was positive because it meant that I was making spiritual progress. I was getting a glimpse of my own wrongdoing in the increasingly obvious contrast between my lifestyle and Leslie's. Yes, it's difficult for the spouse to cope with, but perhaps there can be a nugget of hope in knowing that the journey to God is a turbulent experience for some people.

It's equally critical to be aware that your unbelieving partner probably doesn't comprehend what's happening to him. Most men aren't in touch with their feelings anyway, and so when their emotions go a little haywire, it really confounds them. Asking them to engage in a rational conversation about the matter can be seen as a threat because they're afraid to delve into the uncharted territory of their feelings.

UNDERSTANDING HER MINDSET

Of course, Leslie was going through her own emotional turmoil at the time. Actually, she was feeling the same kind of emotions I was, except for totally different reasons.

For instance, she felt hurt and angry, too, but it was because of the way I belittled her faith and walked around with such a self-righteous demeanor, especially in the first few months after she became a Christian.

While I professed tolerance for her newfound faith, my unspoken attitude toward her was, "What do you have to go to church for? What's wrong with you that you need that kind of crutch?" It made her angry that I could be so open-minded about most things, but when it came to Christianity, my mind slammed shut.

And Leslie felt frustrated because now there was something extremely important to her—her relationship with Jesus Christ—that she couldn't share with me. It was the first time since we were fourteen years old that she was going through something that we couldn't experience together.

For instance, during this time period our finances were a mess, and this was creating considerable anxiety in our relationship. So late one afternoon Leslie went into our bedroom, reclined on the bed, and started studying the Bible in a search for answers.

As she read, she began to experience in a fresh way how much God loved her. She was coming to understand that God really did have a heart to ease her anxiety and to infuse her with peace. As a sense of gratitude and awe welled up inside of her, she began to weep. She was just so happy that there was a God who wanted to help her even as a good father helps a treasured child.

But then she glanced out the window and saw that I was arriving home from work. Quickly, she scrambled to hide the Bible under the bed because she knew that if I saw it, I'd probably use it as an excuse to pick a fight. She had to dry her tears, stuff her emotions deep down inside of her, and emerge from the bedroom as if nothing had happened.

She had just caught a wonderful glimpse of God's love, and it was so meaningful to her that she had been moved to tears, yet she couldn't breathe a word of it to the person she loved the most. That was extremely frustrating to her.

As she grew spiritually, this kind of thing happened time and time again. She'd learn a new spiritual insight and have no husband to share it with. She'd feel a powerful desire to worship God, but she knew better than to mention anything about it to me. She'd receive an answer to prayer, yet she knew I'd only scoff at it if she told me. She'd meet Christians who would make great friends for us but hesitated to introduce us because of the church connection.

It was as if she were visiting a wonderful city, drinking in all sorts of terrific sights and sounds, but I wasn't interested in coming along with her or hearing about it. The resulting sense of isolation fed her frustration.

And Leslie felt fear, too. Fear about the future. She looked down the road of our marriage and winced because she could see it would be paved with conflict all the way to the horizon—disagreements over how to raise the kids, how to spend our money, how to spend our weekends, and on and on.

Even more than that, she felt afraid of what was going to happen at the end of the road. She knew that someday I would stand before a Holy God who would say to me, "Lee, you chose to be separate from Me all your life, and I let you have your own way. Now you can have your way throughout all eternity by being separated from Me forever." She loved me, and she knew I was headed for a day of reckoning.

Can you see how a spiritual mismatch can ignite a powder

keg of emotions in both spouses? No wonder God lovingly looked out for our best interests by warning us in Scripture: "Do not be yoked together with unbelievers."[1]

He wasn't trying to ruin anyone's fun or arbitrarily narrow the field of potential spouses by eliminating those who aren't Christians. He wasn't saying that unbelievers don't matter or that they don't know how to love other people. He was merely trying to protect both parties in the relationship from the explosion of emotions that can decimate an unbalanced marriage.

If you're single and considering marriage, I hope that you hear God clearly on this. He's saying, "I love you so much and I want so intensely for our relationship to flourish that you must understand this: *A spiritual mismatch spells trouble.* It will stifle your spiritual growth and frustrate both you and your spouse."

It's easy for our judgment to be clouded by love. After I gave a forty-minute message on this topic, a young woman came up to me and said, "I'm dating a man who is checking out Christianity, and I just know he's going to become a Christian before too long. So don't you think it would be all right for us to get married? Really, it's just a matter of time before he makes a commitment to Christ."

I wanted to say: "Read my lips: 'Do not be yoked together with unbelievers!' For his sake, for your own sake—heed God's Word!"

But so many Christians are already unequally yoked with an unbeliever. Maybe your partner led you to believe he was a Christian before your marriage by mouthing the right words and putting on a good act, and you've come to discover too late that he was only trying to succeed in the courtship.

"I met my husband at a Christian college—of course I thought he was a believer," one woman told me. "He knew the lingo, he grew up in the church, but after we got married, he shut the door to spiritual matters. It was okay with him if I grew spiritually, but what kind of life is that for me?"

Or maybe you're like Leslie, who became a Christian after

the wedding. Whatever the reason for you being in this situation, you need to take this to heart: *God isn't going to abandon you*. He will offer you wisdom on how to survive.

That's what Leslie found. She followed four basic pieces of biblical advice, and it saved our marriage. In fact, the word that Leslie uttered the most during this troubled era was, "Help!" She needed God's assistance to get through life day by day. So let's take that word and use each letter—H, E, L, P—to represent one bit of biblical counsel to assist you in getting through these turbulent times. For instance, the "H" in help stands for this advice:

• **Harness the support of others.**

The Old Testament says, "Two are better than one, because they have a good return for their work: If one falls down, his friend can help him up. But pity the man who falls and has no one to help him up!"[2]

Leslie realized from the outset that she couldn't get through this alone. It was clear to her that she needed someone else's guidance and support, especially because she was a new Christian who was still trying to sort through what the faith was all about. So she built into her friendship with a mature Christian named Linda, the woman who had led her to Christ.

Basically, Linda served Leslie in two areas. First, she helped Leslie grow in her faith, which was important because I certainly wasn't any help in that area. In fact, I was discouraging Leslie. Unfortunately, some Christians in a mismatched marriage find that their faith becomes stagnant because their relationship with their spouse has stifled their spiritual growth and they aren't connected with anyone to help them get past spiritual infancy toward spiritual adulthood.

The second thing Linda offered was godly advice, consistent prayers, and a shoulder to cry on. But as important as what Linda offered was *how* she offered it.

For instance, Linda made sure that Leslie didn't get mired

in self-pity or fall into the trap of being judgmental and negative toward me. It would have been easy when Linda and Leslie got together for the conversation to turn into a bitter gripe session about my latest misbehavior.

Leslie could have developed a mindset that said, "It's you and me and God against Lee." That sort of attitude would have eventually leaked into our relationship and poisoned it. Linda insisted that Leslie focus on the good aspects of my behavior and character as much as possible.

Linda also made sure that Leslie didn't start blaming every little problem in our marriage on the fact that I wasn't a Christian. It's easy to say, "If he would just become a Christian, everything would be perfect. He'd help around the house without complaining, he'd always control his temper, he'd always put my interests first, and he'd automatically stop working so much at the office."

That's just not reality. Christian marriages aren't perfect, no matter what image people try to project. It was important for Linda to keep reminding Leslie of that whenever Leslie would begin idealizing marriage to a believer. Not *all* of my shortcomings were directly attributable to my spiritual condition.

What Linda did was to keep Leslie focused on God, not on her situation. She encouraged Leslie to keep building on the common ground that she and I still shared, so that we wouldn't drift apart. And she helped Leslie maintain a biblical perspective toward marriage and toward me.

If you're married to an unbeliever, do you have someone like Linda in your life? Are you close friends with a mature Christian who can give you support, guidance, and encouragement? Leslie will tell you how critically important it is to link up with someone you can pour out your heart to and pray with on an ongoing basis.

The "E" in the word "Help" stands for this advice:

• **Exercise restraint**

Believe me, Leslie's ability to restrain herself from trying to stuff Christianity down my throat was a major reason that our relationship remained intact.

Leslie stayed sensitive to how controversial Christianity was to me. The apostle Peter said we should be ready to defend our faith at all times, but he also added an important caveat. We're to do so "with gentleness and respect."[3]

Leslie respected me enough to give me some space. Even though there were times when she wanted to whack me over the head with a Bible, tie me up and force me to listen to a tape of a sermon, or drag me to church by my hair, she exercised restraint.

Admittedly, she did go a little far at times. For instance, if she found a Christian book that she thought would benefit me, she would open it to the appropriate page and leave it on the coffee table. Sometimes it would sit there for a week or more. That was all right with me because I usually ignored it.

In other words, she didn't go overboard. If she had taped Bible verses to my mirror in the morning, stuffed tracts into my socks when I was packing for a trip, kept resetting my car stereo to a Christian station, or hung crosses all over the house, it certainly would have only heightened the tension.

And Leslie restrained herself from getting too deeply involved with church when it would injure our relationship. We reached an accommodation where it was all right with me if she went to church on Sundays, but if she had been out several nights a week at prayer meetings, seminars, or small groups, I would have said, "Time out! Something's got to change! This is controlling your life."

Mostly, she relied on her Bible study with Linda for her spiritual growth, because they could get together during the day when I was at work.

In addition, when Leslie met alone with God every day, it was always early in the morning. I get up later than she, and the first thing I would see as I walked into the kitchen for breakfast was Leslie closing her Bible. It was as if she were saying: "I've met with God and received my daily spiritual input; now, let's not let this issue get between us today."

Perhaps the most important way Leslie exercised restraint was that she didn't nit-pick everything I did. She didn't heap guilt on me every time I would have a few drinks or let loose with some bad language. She didn't refuse to go to parties or to movies where the language might be a little offensive. While she did hold her ground on important issues, she didn't elevate every little thing into a spiritual battle.

Can you see why exercising restraint did so much to preserve our marriage? I've met many spiritually mismatched Christians who struggle with how far to push because they feel so impassioned about wanting to reach their partner with the Gospel. But much of what they do can be counter-productive. They can inadvertently inflame their partner's emotions or prompt them to stubbornly dig in their heels.

Let me add that this is an area where general advice is difficult because of the unique personality dynamics of each marriage. That's why it's so important to get one-on-one advice from a mature and discerning Christian friend.

The next letter in "Help" is "L," which stands for:

• **Live out your faith, don't just talk it.**

By that, I mean that the integrity of your everyday life as a Christian will speak more powerfully to your spouse than any sermon you can preach.

Talking to Christians in the first century, Peter said that even if your spouse won't listen when you're talking to him about God, he will respond to your respectful and godly behavior.[4]

As a new believer, Leslie wasn't ready yet to answer the skeptical and often hostile questions I had about the faith. If she had tried to debate me about God, the conversation probably would have degenerated into a fruitless argument. If she had moralized and started quoting Scripture to me, I would have walked out of the room.

But she did something more effective. She cooperated with God as He changed her character, attitude, and outlook. She yielded herself as fully as she could as God began molding her into a more Christ-like person.

I watched as she increasingly became a person of humility, integrity, love, and self-sacrifice. And, in the end, the main reason I was willing to take an open-minded look at the Christian faith was because I was astonished by how Leslie was being transformed into a better person.

Besides, Leslie's decision to live out her faith in front of me had many positive effects on our marriage. Jo Berry, who has researched spiritually mismatched marriages, said this: "Rather than wishing things were different, all of us have to admit that, for the most part, our marriages only will be as good or as bad as we make them. Any unequally yoked wife can have a 'Christian' marriage to the extent that she is willing to implement God's standards into her performance and the relationship itself."[5]

That's a great insight. What she's saying is that unequally yoked wives and husbands can make their marriage "Christian" as far as they're willing, unilaterally, to live out what it means for them to be a follower of Christ.

The Bible contains wonderful advice on how spouses should behave, and when one partner follows that biblical approach as much as possible, the long-term effect on the marriage is going to be positive.

And, finally, the "P" in "Help" stands for this advice:

• **Pray, pray, and pray.**

There is power in prayer, and besides, when you're in the grip of feeling hurt, frustrated, angry, and afraid, who but God can really help?

I mentioned in an earlier chapter that Leslie often focused

her prayers on this Old Testament verse: "I will give you a new heart and put a new spirit in you; I will remove from you your heart of stone and give you a heart of flesh."[6]

She would often say to God: "Lord, Lee's heart is like granite, and I can't seem to crack it open. But I know You love him more than I do, and You have the power to do a spiritual heart-transplant. Lord, please, give him a new heart and a new spirit, because only You can do it."

And she went to God and said, "Your Word promises that if I ask for wisdom, You'll give it. Lord, give me the wisdom to know how far to push and when to back off. I don't want to alienate Lee; I want to cooperate with You in reaching him."

She received God's comfort during periods when I was especially obnoxious, and she obtained God's power to love me during times when, frankly, I wasn't very loveable.

And do you know what happened? *God used this difficult time to mold Leslie into someone she never would have become without it.*

It was during this turbulent era of our marriage that she learned how to pour herself out in authentic, heartfelt prayer. Formula praying didn't cut it; she needed to express her deepest feelings to God. She needed to bring Him her anger, frustration, and pain, and that meant that her prayers weren't always polite or fancy. Sometimes they were messy and tear-stained.

Through these times, she learned to be dependent on God and to wait on His timing, even when she wanted desperately to take matters into her own hands. She learned how to forgive someone who was hard to forgive, and she was taught lessons of perseverance and hope.

Today, she still inspires me with her life of prayer and faith. I'm sorry that I put her through such difficult times, but I praise God for the way He took those circumstances and used them to impact her positively—and, through her, to influence many others.

It's interesting that more than thirty years ago, researchers studied 413 high-achieving people to figure out what they had in common. Guess what they found? Nearly all of them had been forced to overcome very difficult obstacles to become who they were.[7] Going through those difficult times stretched them into becoming something they may never have become otherwise.

That's a fitting analogy for what God can do. He can take a person's heart-breaking experience of living with an unbeliever and mold him or her into someone whose faith has a depth, a character, and a quality it would never have had.

If you're spiritually mismatched, this isn't a wasted time of your life. God can use it to mature you in your faith in ways that will, in the end, benefit you and others. The apostle Paul was well-acquainted with trials and tribulations. Listen to what he wrote on the topic:

"We also rejoice in our sufferings, because we know that suffering produces perseverance; perseverance, character; and character, hope. And hope does not disappoint us, because God has poured out his love into our hearts by the Holy Spirit, whom he has given us."[8]

For Leslie and me, our spiritual mismatch had a wonderful ending. We thought we were happily married before we were followers of Christ, but now we know the heights that a relationship can reach when both partners make Christ the center of the marriage.

It's as if God said to us: "You used to relate to each other on an emotional level, an intellectual level, and a physical level, and all of that was fine. However, that's just part of what it means to live as husband and wife. Now you're going to relate on a spiritual level as well, and there's no greater or more daring intimacy than sharing your souls with each other and with Me."

But let's face it, every husband and wife won't end up together in God's kingdom. I know a woman who has been married to an unbelieving husband for sixteen years, and he only recently agreed to come to church with her for the first time. That single step was the culmination of sixteen years of praying, hoping, and dreaming. Unfortunately, some husbands and wives will see their partners go to their grave without ever having received Christ as their forgiver and leader. That's a sobering reality.

Yet please grab onto this truth—*You are not responsible for your spouse's eternity*. It's crucial for both you and your partner to understand that. You will not be held accountable by God if your spouse rejects Christ all the way to the grave. Husbands and wives are responsible for their own choices.

So don't let misplaced guilt wear you down. Don't let your actions be driven by an inappropriate sense of responsibility for your spouse's spiritual state, because inevitably that will cause you to cross the bounds of pushing too hard for his conversion.

No, your responsibility is for you to live out your life, as best you can, in a Christ-honoring way. As my friend Don Cousins likes to say, "If you honor God with your everyday life, He'll honor you for a lifetime."

Even in the midst of a spiritual mismatch.

10

HELPING YOUR CHURCH CONNECT WITH UNCHURCHED HARRY AND MARY

The advertisement in the weekend newspaper showed a sophisticated businessman leaning casually against the grille of his Rolls Royce. His chauffeur and beautiful brick mansion were in the background. The caption said: "Where Do You Turn When Something's Still Missing After You've Got It All?"

Then the ad provided the answer: the name of an evangelical church, which listed its Sunday service times.

This is great! I thought to myself. *Here's a church where people have gotten together to create a service that will be relevant to a group that a lot of churches miss—financially successful unchurched Harrys and Marys.* Knowing that wealthy, independent, and worldly individuals can be among the hardest to reach with the Gospel, I felt encouraged and decided to visit the church.

Unfortunately, I found what I encounter far too often: an environment that would have been an instant turn-off to the very people these well-meaning Christians were attempting to reach.

The service started with someone's asking the congregation to sing along with a chorus for which no lyrics were provided. Regular attenders, of course, knew the words, but I felt awkward. Other hymns, accompanied by an organ, dated from 1869, 1871, and 1874, with such lyrics as, "Heav'nly portals loud with hosannas ring." The microphones were tinny and the sound tended to cut in and out, prompting a vocalist at one point to pause with an embarrassed smile in the middle of a song.

During the announcement time, a pastor directed new-comers to fill out a card "so we can put you on our mailing list." He also jokingly but with an air of desperation offered a $100 bounty if members of the church's board would attend a meeting that afternoon so they would finally have a quorum. He added with frustration, "We need to approve the painting of the church, which should have been done last year, and the painting of the house I live in, which should have been painted last year, too."

The sermon, part of a series called "Issues in Christian Discipleship," quoted some experts, but they were all leaders of that denomination. The pastor talked about denying oneself to follow Christ, but there wasn't much explanation of what that meant on a practical, day-to-day level. He did say the Christian life has its benefits, although he didn't elaborate on what they were. At the conclusion, he offered only two steps for people to take: Either turn over your life to Christ or commit yourself to deeper discipleship.

As I was trying to leave the sanctuary, someone near the door grabbed my hand, pumped it in a friendly handshake, and asked my name. He didn't seem to want to let go until I identified myself.

Were these Christians doing anything inherently wrong? Of course not. I'm sure they were good, well-intentioned people who had a genuine desire to communicate the Gospel to unchurched people.

But were they really creating a service that would address

the needs, concerns, and longings of irreligious individuals? No, they weren't. By just doing church the way it always had been done, they had created an atmosphere where *they* felt comfortable but which would have chased away unchurched people like the businessman in their ad.

In fact, if you were the friend of a successful executive and you brought him to that church, the evangelism process may have been disrupted rather than promoted. His reaction might have been, "Why should I take anything seriously from a inefficiently run and outdated place like this?"

Think about the signals he would have picked up. He would have felt like an outsider when he was asked to sing an unfamiliar song without printed lyrics. Singing hymns with odd and antiquated language would have suggested that the place was out of touch. After all, to a modern secular person, what's a "hosanna" and a "heav'nly portal"?

The bad sound system and the "bounty" for board members would have told him this was a poorly run organization with an uncommitted core and a tolerance for sloppy operations—things that the businessman would never tolerate in his own organization.

The comment about painting the church and pastor's house would have made him uncomfortable by hinting at behind-the-scenes tension at the church. The direction to fill out a card so he could get on a mailing list would have created anxiety because he would figure he'd probably get a visitor knocking at his door or a mailbox full of pleas for him to return.

The sermon title would have baffled him because he wouldn't understand the word "discipleship," and even if he had, it wouldn't have applied to him since he's not a disciple. The quoting of denominational leaders would have told him this was an inbred organization that doesn't look beyond its own borders and is probably out of sync with experts from the "real world."

The call to commit himself to Christ most likely would have seemed premature and presumptuous. The questions he harbored about Christianity seemingly didn't matter to the church. And the handshake by the usher would have prompted concerns that he was going to get roped into an uncomfortable conversation with a stranger—in fact, probably one of those "born-again types."

SELECTING YOUR HARRYS AND MARYS

I've been seeing more and more of this phenomenon around the country. Many Christians are sincerely concerned about reaching Unchurched Harry and Mary, but they're not sure how to go about doing it.

Instead of thinking through how to produce an appropriate kind of service or event, they buy prepackaged advertisements to try to bring unchurched people their way. And yet even if the ads do attract unchurched people, the service would most likely confirm to them why they stopped going to church in the first place.

Unless Christians make a conscious effort to create programs that will appeal to unbelievers, they naturally default to designing events that reflect their own tastes. Just as the apostle Paul said he became "all things to all men so that by all possible means I might save some,"[1] Christians today must strategically think through how to present the Gospel in an environment that will attract those who are in need of it.

But let me emphatically add that I'm not suggesting anybody alter the Gospel to make it artificially attractive to unchurched people. Watering it down or eliminating the difficult elements of sin or repentance is totally unacceptable.

In fact, theologian William Hordern has proposed a helpful distinction between "transforming" the Gospel and "translating" it.[2] Those who transform it are improperly trying to turn the Gospel into something it isn't in order to make it more palatable to the unchurched. But those who translate it are keeping the message intact while merely using different modes to communicate it in ways that connect with the people they are trying to reach.

Just as the New Testament originally was written in everyday Greek so people would be able to understand it, these Christians try to translate the Gospel into the everyday language and art forms of twentieth-century America. That's not only legitimate but it's biblical, and I believe it's the only way churches today are going to meaningfully penetrate our stubbornly secular society.

However, Christians can't speak the language of the people they're trying to reach until they know who their target audience is going to be. How the Gospel is communicated in the inner city, for example, is going to be different from how it is communicated in affluent suburbs, because musical tastes and life experiences are different.

When consulting with churches, Jim Dethmer asks them to clarify what business they are in. Willow Creek Community Church, for example, has written its mission statement this way: "To turn irreligious people into fully devoted followers of Jesus Christ." Basically, that's a restatement of the Great Commission that Jesus gave His followers: "Therefore go and make disciples of all nations, baptizing them in the name of the Father and of the Son and of the Holy Spirit, and teaching them to obey everything I have commanded you."[3]

While that goal is shared by most churches, the next critically important question Dethmer asks is: "What raw material are you starting with?"[4] The answer to that inquiry will largely shape the way a church fulfills its ministry.

In other words, some churches are seeking to reach *unchurched non-Christians* and turn them into devoted followers of Christ. These "seeker-driven" churches must fashion their ministry in a way that brings in and effectively speaks to secular individuals. Examples include Buckhead Community Church in Atlanta, Christ Community Church outside Chicago, Kensington Community Church near Detroit, Horizons Community

Church in the Los Angeles area, and the Waterfront Church in Southampton, England.

Their approach is going to be different from that of a church that decides its main mission field will be *unchurched Christians*. For instance, Eastside Foursquare Church in Kirkland, Washington, is primarily focused on reaching "nominal Christians," which it defines as "those who claim to be born again, but are not committed to any church." Pastor Doug Murren believes as many as a third of the residents near his church fall into that category.[5] (Nationally, 44% of unchurched people claim to have made a commitment to Jesus Christ.[6]) Secondarily, Murren is trying to reach unchurched non-Christians.

Churches seeking to bring in unchurched Christians are more likely to use worship as an element of outreach because this connects with their target audience. In contrast, some irreligious people, like Leslie and me when we were unchurched, aren't comfortable in worship settings because they find it difficult to praise a God they don't believe in.

Different still would be a church trying to reach *churched unbelievers*, which would be individuals who attend a place of worship but for whatever reason remain untouched by the Gospel. Perhaps they are in a denomination that fails to proclaim the historic Gospel message. One study said this is the most reachable of all groups in the U.S.[7]

Then there are churches whose main target, whether they want to admit it or not, is *churched Christians*. Through superior programs or teaching, they grow by drawing believers out of other congregations in their area.

HITTING THE BULL'S-EYE

Even beyond that, churches that are successful in reaching unchurched people focus on particular age groups. Murren's church, for example, is known for its ability to minister to baby boomers, or people born between 1946 and 1964. Calvary Church Newport Mesa in Costa Mesa, California, and New Song Church in Walnut, California, (whose slogan is, "where the flock likes to rock") have targeted baby busters, or those born immediately after the boomers. Consequently, their styles of ministry and music are significantly different from each other, but each is well-tailored for the appropriate target group.

Some churches purposefully go after unchurched men. Their music selection, dramas, and use of sermon illustrations appeal to a male perspective. Yes, they also want to reach unchurched women, but they find that men generally are more antagonistic toward the Gospel. By going after the more resistant gender, they find that they are also successful in reaching women. The reverse, however, isn't necessarily true. If they were to create services that would appeal primarily to women, the men may not respond.

Saddleback Valley Community Church in California has gone so far as to prepare a detailed profile of the person the church is targeting. Reminiscent of "Unchurched Harry," Saddleback talks about "Saddleback Sam," who is:

". . . a well-educated young urban professional. He is self-satisfied, and comfortable with his life. He likes his job and where he lives. He is affluent, recreation conscious, and prefers the casual and informal over the formal. He is interested in health and fitness, and he thinks he is enjoying life more than 5 years ago, but he is overextended in time and money, and is stressed out. He has some religious background from childhood, but he hasn't been to church for 15 or 20 years, and he is skeptical of 'organized religion.' He doesn't want to be recognized when he comes to church."[8]

Using a term like "target audience" causes some Christians to wince because it sounds like a cold marketing approach. Isn't it true that we want to reach *everyone* with the Gospel? Said Dethmer: "The reality is that we *can't* reach them all, and if we try to reach them all equally, we won't reach any successfully."[9]

"Is it legitimate to address deliberately a particular segment of our population? My response to that question is, 'Of course! Every missionary targets his audience,'" Murren writes. "After all, if you don't know whom God has called you to reach, how can you possibly establish a strategy for reaching them? Clearly defining your target group, therefore, is not only essential to your philosophy of ministry but also vital in ensuring your effectiveness as a successful pastor in a greatly unchurched culture."[10]

Once the bull's-eye of a target audience is defined, the next step is to determine how to get the arrow there. That means developing a workable strategy for reaching that group. How will Christians in that church successfully connect with the people whom God is calling them to reach?

Perhaps it will be based on direct-mail advertising; maybe it will focus on a more relational approach in which Christians will build friendships with unchurched people and invite them to services for seekers. Those services could be weekly, monthly, or quarterly. Perhaps concerts could be used to bring in secular people and expose them to the church. Or periodic events for seekers, such as men's breakfasts, women's brunches, or evangelistic dinner parties, can be strategically scheduled during the year. A variety of approaches are possible.

Among churches that specifically try to reach unchurched unbelievers, a seven-step strategy is often used:

1. Believing Bob builds an authentic relationship with Unchurched Harry.

2. Believing Bob tells Unchurched Harry how God has changed his life and, to the best of his ability, seeks to communicate the Gospel over time.

3. Believing Bob invites Unchurched Harry to a service designed for seekers and answers his questions and concerns.

4. Once Harry commits himself to Christ, he begins attending a worship service geared for believers.

5. Harry joins a small group designed to help him grow spiritually.

6. Harry discovers, develops, and deploys his spiritual gift in order to honor God and to build the church.

7. Harry begins stewarding his resources—time and money—in a godly fashion.

Then the cycle is repeated, with Now-Churched Harry building a relationship with Unchurched Larry.[11]

Whatever strategy is chosen, it should influence every aspect of the ministry. It should drive what kind of building is rented or constructed, what sort of music is used, what kind of drama or multi-media are employed, the titles and illustrations in messages, the design and contents of the bulletin, the manner in which ushers greet visitors, the way the parking lot is handled, the way the grounds are kept, the times of the services, the way participants are dressed, and on and on.

All of this may sound difficult to implement, but it becomes much easier when it flows out of heartfelt values that result when key leaders of the church maintain close relationships with the kind of unchurched people who make up the target audience.

When they're regularly hanging around with Unchurched Harry and Mary, talking with them over dinner or going out to movies with them, they naturally get to know the kind of approach that will attract or repel them. A simple way to determine what kind of service or event to create is to ask, "What would Harry and Mary think of this? Would I feel comfortable and confident bringing them to something like this?"

Unfortunately, many Christians who say they want to bring the Gospel to the unchurched of their community don't actually know any irreligious people. To them, Unchurched Harry and Mary are faceless entities with mysterious patterns of behavior. As a result, they end up inadvertently creating a church service or event more to their own tastes than to that of their target audience.

TALKING TO THE CUSTOMER

One way many churches have gained a broader understanding of the unchurched in their area is to conduct a community survey. Typically, volunteers go to homes in the neighborhood and ask residents whether they actively attend a local church. If they do, they thank him and go to the next house. If they don't, they ask why. Nuances of the results vary region by region, but I've always been fascinated by the general consistency of these surveys.

When one neighborhood canvass was conducted in suburban Chicago in 1975, these were the top reasons people gave for steering clear of church:

• Churches are always asking for money, yet nothing of personal value ever seems to happen with the funds.

• Church services are boring and lifeless.

• Church services are predictable.

• Sermons are irrelevant to daily life in the "real world."

• The pastor makes people feel guilty and ignorant, so that people leave church feeling worse than when they arrived.[12]

More than a decade later, a survey of eight hundred people in another U.S. urban area yielded similar responses for why people skipped church:

• Church people are cold and unfriendly.

• Sermons are boring and don't relate to real life.

• Going to church is a guilt trip.

• Churches don't care about you, all they want is your money.

• We're too busy; going to church is a waste of time.[13]

A door-to-door survey was conducted in southern England in 1990. What the respondents said can be paraphrased this way: "We are busy people with busy lives, and nothing about Christianity persuades us to give up what we do on a Sunday. We've got better things to do than to participate in an irrelevant and empty experience."[14]

Actually, these survey results should be encouraging to Christians. The reason is that with some prayer, planning, and creativity, these complaints can be overcome without in any way compromising the Gospel.

In other words, these objections generally relate to the method that's used to communicate the Gospel, not to the message itself, and consequently we're free to use our God-given creativity to present Christ's message in new ways that our target audience will connect with. As the apostle Paul told the Christians at the first-century church in Colosse: "Be wise in the way you act toward outsiders; make the most of every opportunity."[15]

So instead of services that are boring, lifeless, and predictable, they can be designed to reflect the excitement, adventure, and, yes, even the sacrifice of Christianity. They can vary from week to week rather than being stuck in the same programming rut. Instead of using heavy-handed fund-raising appeals, they can teach their believers responsible biblical stewardship but exempt visitors from giving. Instead of ethereal sermons unrelated to daily living, messages can be practical and application-oriented.

Rather than being cold and unfriendly, churches can be warm and inclusive toward outsiders without smothering them. Instead of relying on guilt tactics, they can present a balanced picture of the faith that includes God's grace, forgiveness, and love, while still teaching about the reality of sin and the need for personal repentance.

Keep in mind there are at least fifty-five million unchurched adults in the country. Think how many might return to church if it were only more sensitive to their needs and relevant to their lives.

But how is this going to happen unless individual Christians make the decision to strategically team up with their church to turbo-charge their evangelistic efforts? They ought to be partners who are committed to assisting each other in the ongoing adventure of penetrating their community with the Gospel.

For too long, their efforts have been disjointed. Many Christians feel like "Lone Rangers" who must stumble through the evangelism process on their own. Meanwhile, church leaders wonder why their pews are filled with the same faces week after week, and why so few new believers are being baptized.

But think of the potential to make inroads for God's kingdom if churches would actively assist their believers by providing safe places where they can bring their friends to hear the challenging message of Christ.

What about you and your church? You have important roles to play. First, you can personally influence the Unchurched Harrys and Marys in your sphere of relationships. And, second, you can encourage and assist your church in understanding the mindset of irreligious people so effective events, programs, and services can be implemented.

These next few chapters, which are based on what attracted me to church and kept me coming back until I made a commitment to Christ, will give you some ideas for creating evangelistic opportunities.

11

"GIMME SOME SPACE"

When I walked into a church service to check out the Christian faith, I was armed and ready. Concealed inside my sports coat was a secret weapon, and as long as I carried it I felt protected.

No, it wasn't a gun; it was a reporter's notebook, the kind *The Chicago Tribune* issues to its writers. The reason it gave me security was that if I encountered someone I knew, I could whip it out and say, "Oh, I'm not really attending here; I'm thinking of doing a story on this place. You know, there's probably a scandal around here somewhere."

That gives you a taste of how self-conscious Unchurched Harry and Mary can be when they venture inside a church. It would be comparable to the feeling that a Christian would have if he walked into a Moslem mosque for the first time. He wouldn't want to be highlighted or pointed out because he would be embarrassed and, besides, what if the neighbor down the block saw him and thought that he was converting! That's how many unchurched people feel when they take that monumental step of entering a church.

Most Christians underestimate the tension and anxiety that Unchurched Harry and Mary experience when they walk through the church door. To a Christian, church is a comfortable home, a place populated by like-minded people who share a love for Christ. But for unchurched people, it's a foreboding place of the unexpected and unusual.

They're afraid of doing something wrong—staying seated when everybody else responds to an unspoken cue and rises to their feet; being unable to locate a Bible verse that everyone else has quickly found; or singing off-key as they try to negotiate the arcane melody of an eighteenth-century hymn. They don't want to draw attention to themselves through some inadvertent gaffe.

That's why when Unchurched Harry and Mary come to church, their number-one value is anonymity. As much as possible, they want to blend in with the crowd.

In fact, the more secularized a community is, the more important anonymity becomes, because it's less socially acceptable to be seen by neighbors and business associates in a church. For instance, anonymity is especially important for churches in the West and Northwest, where church membership is lowest, and somewhat less crucial in the South, where church involvement is at its highest.

In contrast, when a Christian visits another church, one of his highest priorities is friendliness. He wants to be recognized and greeted by other members of God's family, and because he feels that way, he often incorrectly assumes that Unchurched Harry and Mary want the same thing in their church experience.

A few years ago I was vacationing in Florida with my family, and on Sunday we visited an evangelical congregation. In the middle of the service, the pastor asked any visitors to stand and introduce themselves. He thought he was being friendly by welcoming newcomers, but the truth is that most people are scared to death of speaking in public under any circumstances, and that's accentuated in unchurched people who are already uncomfortable about being inside a sanctuary. It didn't surprise me that we were the only visiting family among the four hundred people in attendance that Sunday.

Studies show that no matter how well-intentioned the congregation, most church visitors don't want to be identified during the service. What's more, a majority don't want to wear name tags or have anyone visit them in their home the following week.[1] Yet this is precisely the approach many churches take toward their visitors because Christians think they want an outpouring of friendliness.

ADVANTAGES OF ANONYMITY

Anonymity does two crucial things for Unchurched Harry and Mary. First, it preserves their *control*. When I first went to church, I wanted to maintain as much control of the situation as I could because this gave me security. For instance, Leslie's friends, Linda and Jerry, offered to drive us to church, but I wanted to take our own car. That way, I could sneak out and make a fast getaway if something went awry. I was glad that the church I chose to visit was attracting lots of people to its services so that I could just become another face in the crowd.

I knew that if I wanted information about the church or I had a question, I could go up to someone and I would get a warm and helpful response, but this is important: *I wanted to be the one to initiate contact*.

And I was grateful that nobody sidled up next to me, shook my hand, and invited me over to his house for Sunday dinner. One of my biggest hesitations in going to church was that I might get locked into a conversation with an evangelistic zealot who would probe me with spiritual questions that I wasn't ready to answer.

Second, anonymity gives *time* to Unchurched Harry and Mary. It creates a safe environment for them to seek after the truth about Christ at their own pace. Once they discover that they can relax in a church and not be intimidated or embarrassed, they're much more willing to keep coming back even as the messages challenge them to their core.

And as we've said, evangelism is most often a process, with the Holy Spirit working over a period of time. In my case, after initially visiting a church in January 1980, I felt comfortable enough to return almost weekly for nearly two years while I systematically checked out the faith. Most of the time I sat in the back (close to an exit in case anything weird happened) and kept to myself, but the whole time I was soaking in spiritual truth.

The tightrope a church must walk in handling unchurched visitors is to allow adequate anonymity without making it seem as though the church is cold and uncaring. This is especially true of churches in the South, where there's a higher cultural expectation of warm hospitality.

One church took the approach of training its ushers to watch the eyes of people who entered the lobby. If the visitor was looking around as if lost and wanting assistance, the usher would step forward to make contact and ask politely if he could help. But if the visitor purposefully avoided making eye contact, the usher would let him go by, giving him a friendly smile and maybe a "good morning" but would not intercept him. As for me, when I entered the movie theater where church was being held that first Sunday, I was emitting body language that screamed, "Leave me alone!" I'm glad people heeded my signal.

Also, many churches have established ways for visitors to request information when they want it rather than foisting material on them. Some have a tear-off card as part of their Sunday bulletin, allowing anyone who wants information to fill it out and put it in the offering basket. They can check boxes relating to the nature of their question or inquiry.

Their attention is directed to the card by the person making announcements during the service, although no pressure is exerted on them to fill one out. The reason is that many unchurched visitors dread getting on a mailing list or receiving a visit from a pastor. Being forced to provide their name strips away some of their control and makes them feel vulnerable. After all, who knows what happens after your name gets into somebody's computer?

Preserving anonymity can be especially difficult in small churches. When only a handful of people attend, it's inevitable that a new person will stand out. One midwest church that was created to reach the unchurched purposefully waited until its core group grew to over one hundred people before it began services targeted to seekers. That way, a visitor was more likely to feel inconspicuous.

Other churches periodically teach their core about the attitudes of the unchurched so that their congregation is sensitized to how Unchurched Harry and Mary feel. That way, the members understand the reasons behind why they shouldn't make too big of a fuss over a new face among them.

Even a small church can assimilate Harry and Mary in a nonthreatening way by:
• being friendly but not overbearing;
• being polite but not fawning;
• courteously greeting them but not engaging them in a conversation that they have difficulty extricating themselves from.

One church chose a theater as its meeting place specifically because the audience lights could be easily dimmed, which would give a sense of security to the unchurched.

Some churches offer an informal reception for visitors after the service. There are some unchurched people who are willing to attend such a reception.[2] The key, however, is to clearly make them optional so that visitors don't feel any pressure to participate. That way, those who don't want to forfeit their anonymity can retain control.

Courteously offering visitors information about the church with no strings attached is fine; in fact, most unchurched people would like this. But keep in mind that a majority of unchurched people don't want any special treatment at your service or event.[3]

Sometimes churches feel as though they give up too much of their own control if they let Unchurched Harry and Mary come and go without getting their name and address. After all, how else can they track people unless they capture that kind of data? How can follow-up be assured? While those are legitimate concerns, that's a sacrifice a church needs to make if it wants to keep attracting the unchurched.

The more an unchurched visitor's anonymity is violated, the more likely that his first visit will be his last. Ideally, the visitor's friend, who brought him to the service in the first place, will be providing informal follow-up and encouraging him to come back for another service.

THE SMALL-GROUP OPTION

At the same time, however, generalizations must be handled carefully. While most unchurched non-believers desire anonymity, there are some who are specifically attracted to an opportunity to interact with Christians. In one study, a significant minority of unchurched people said they would have some level of interest in a seeker-oriented Bible study.[4] Given the increasing desire in our society for meaningful relationships, more and more people might opt for this kind of investigative small group in the future.

A colleague of mine, Garry Poole, has been leading these small groups for years and has always found people to be receptive. Once as a student he transferred from a Christian college to a large state university in Indiana. On a lark, he put up four signs in two dormitories saying that anyone interested in an informal Bible study should call him immediately. He got phone calls from ten people, including eight unbelievers.

175

"I didn't expect non-Christians to call," Garry said. "I guess most Christians were already connected to the Navigators or Campus Crusade, so they weren't interested. But there was a hunger among these unchurched kids for friendship and spiritual discussions."

At their first meeting, Garry said, "If you could ask God any question in the world and He'd answer you, what would it be?" They asked if there was really a hell, why there was so much sickness in the world, whether the Bible really is God's Word, and similar questions. Garry took those issues, did some research, and used one question each week as the topic of conversation. Despite their busy schedules, the unchurched students were faithful in attending, and before leaving the group three of them committed their lives to Christ.

Speaking for myself, I never would have attended a Bible study when I was an unbeliever—I would have been too uncomfortable and afraid of embarrassing myself to discuss spiritual matters with a small number of strangers. Besides, I had enough friends to keep me busy, so I wasn't interested in finding more.

But for others, the group's relational component is a tremendous attraction. That's what Leslie discovered when she invited women in our neighborhood to spend a few hours a week studying the Bible together, using one of many curricula that are available for seeker groups. It was the lure of building better friendships as much as the spiritual component that pulled people into the group.

Even though some unchurched people prefer a relational experience through a small group, they still want to feel safe. They need to be assured that they can freely express their opinions, question the validity of Christian doctrines, and investigate the truth about Christ for as long as they need to come to their own conclusions.

Many churches use evangelistic small groups as a "next step" for Unchurched Harry and Mary. They create a big front door—an evangelistic event or service—at which Unchurched Harry and Mary enjoy anonymity and feel comfortable in absorbing spiritual teaching. After a while the church mentions the availability of small groups for those who are interested. Some select that option, but others who still want to safeguard their identity are still free to return for future large-group events.

"Gimme some space," is the cry of Unchurched Harry and Mary. As Christians, many times we want to shower them with love and acceptance and to enthusiastically tug them down the spiritual path toward Christ. But most of them respond best when we back off enough to provide them with a place where they feel safe to explore what it means to follow Jesus.

12

"GIMME CREATIVITY"

She was a student at the prestigious Harvard Business School, an engaging, sharp-minded woman who also happened to be turned off to church. During class one day she participated in a discussion about excellence in non-profit organizations, and afterward she made an observation about churches that struck me as both depressing and encouraging at the same time.

"It seems to me," she said, "that churches have a big advantage in the area of creativity."

"Why's that?" I asked.

"Because if people went into church with high expectations of what they were going to experience, it would be hard to exceed those expectations and impress them," she said. "But let's be honest—the average person goes to church with extremely low expectations. And so all a church has to do is notch up the creativity just a *little* bit, and it will probably blow 'em away."

What a condemnation of churches! To her, and to many Unchurched Harrys and Marys, church services are considered boring, lifeless, predictable, and dismal. While that's a grossly unfair stereotype in many cases, that opinion persists nonetheless and causes them to steer clear of church.

And yet, that gloomy image offers a terrific opportunity. If unchurched people can somehow be lured back for a service or event, and if the church were to crank up the creativity just a bit, there would be a great potential for positively impacting them.

TAKING OUR CUE FROM GOD

After all, why shouldn't church services be exciting, insightful, daring, creative, awe-inspiring, and celebratory—I mean, isn't that what Christianity is like? Certainly God Himself displayed the ultimate in creativity when He crafted the majestic mountains, the kaleidoscopic array of animal life, the vast beauty of the heavens, the color-splashed forests, the exotic underwater world of the oceans, and the intricate ecosystem that keeps the planet functioning.

And He gave creative gifts to His people. I don't think He wants us to stifle those gifts or leave them dormant. Surely He wants us to express them, especially when we can use that creativity to point out the path to Him. Said Franky Schaeffer:

"As Christians we often speak of men being 'made in God's image.' This formula only remains a set of words until given further meaning and definition. If there is one area that surely sets man clearly apart from the rest of the animal kingdom and gives meaning to these words 'made in the image of God,' it is the area of creativity, the capacity to enjoy beauty, communicate artistically and through abstract ideas. The area of creativity therefore is no minor footnote to the Christian life, but is an essential."[1]

As a movie character named Cool Hand Luke was told, "What we have here is a failure to communicate." Somehow unchurched people have gotten the impression that churches are deadly dull, and from that they conclude Christians and Christianity must be dull and, above all, God must be dull. Friends, they've gotten the wrong idea, and we need to set the record straight.

Let me describe for you the creativity I found when I first began attending a seeker-targeted church. Now, I want to reiterate that all churches don't need to adopt a contemporary approach for seekers every week. I believe that traditional churches are fine as long as they periodically partner with their members to create events to which they can take their un-churched friends. And so these same principles of creativity would apply.

What was it about the creativity that kept me coming back to church as I investigated the claims of Christianity?

• Reason #1: They played my music.

I remember when Leslie was trying to interest me in attending church shortly after she became a Christian. "The music's great," she kept telling me. She would describe it as being "hot" and upbeat, the kind I'd listen to on the radio, but for the longest time, it just didn't sink in with me. I equated churches with droning organ music and dusty hymns. Actually, one reason I finally agreed to visit the church was to find out what in the world she was talking about.

Let's face it: Unchurched people don't spend their spare time listening to organ music, unless they've tuned in an oldies station and happen to hear the 1960s classic "96 Tears" by Question Mark and the Mysterians. Look at what sells in music stores—pop and rock are biggies; classical and gospel music have only modest market shares. And yet most churches highlight classical and organ music.

The reason, of course, is that Christians like that kind of music. Unchurched Harry and Mary, though, have their car radios tuned to more mainstream entertainment. But I can tell you from personal experience that when their favorite style of music is wed to Christian lyrics, the combination can have a strong impact on furthering their spiritual journey.

What we as Christians have to do is crack our society's cultural code. We need to determine what style of music appeals to the Unchurched Harrys and Marys whom we're trying to reach. Are they into rap, country, rock, pop, or jazz? It's easy to determine by checking the ratings and demographics of local radio stations. And once we do that, we can work on harnessing that mode of music for Christ.

As for those who shudder at the thought of modern music in church, baby-boomer expert Doug Murren says, "Relax, the idea of using contemporary music as a means to express worship and outreach isn't as bold or new as it sounds. Did you know that the music to Martin Luther's 'A Mighty Fortress Is Our God' was originally a barroom tune back in the sixteenth century? Also, the great hymns of Charles Wesley were melodic reflections of the nineteenth-century music contemporaneous with his period."[2]

By the way, I've undergone a radical musical conversion in the last few years. I remember when Leslie and I got married, her Scottish mother arranged for a bagpiper to play as we entered the reception. Of course, one song that bagpipers inevitably perform is "Amazing Grace." To me at the time, it was nothing more than a catchy tune.

But years later, at the conclusion of a communion service, we stood to sing "Amazing Grace." Before the song was over, I had to slip underneath the bleachers because I was too embarrassed to have people see me crying so hard. Today that song means the world to me. Now when I sing it, I'm worshiping God for the incredible, undeserved love He's shown me.

As an unchurched person, I loathed old hymns; now, as a Christian, I love them. Often we'll sing them at our worship services—beautiful songs like "How Great Thou Art" and "Great Is Thy Faithfulness"—and they move me emotionally as we use them to praise God. But at services and events designed for unbelievers, we have to determine what music turns their crank, not ours.

• **Reason #2: The unexpected became expected.**

From week to week, I never knew what was going to happen at those church services, and that unpredictability fostered an atmosphere of anticipation among those in attendance. It was sort of like the feeling before a big football game or rock concert. Nobody knew exactly what was going to occur; we just knew that we all were going to experience something that was different and exciting. Before the prelude began, a sense of electricity was already coursing through the crowd.

I remember reading a newspaper article that described a seeker service at a new church. This wasn't a high-tech church with big resources, just 100 people gathered in a rented room. But the writer noted, "There seemed to be quite an expectant buzz in the room before the service." That's what can happen when predictability doesn't lull people into complacency.

• **Reason #3: They connected with the TV generation.**

Baby boomers are the first generation to grow up watching television, and it has shaped the way we process the world. We crave visual stimulation. Rock bands don't just stand up on a stage and perform anymore; today most concerts feature a mixture of video on stacked screens, live-action TV, dramatic staging, and stunning, sweeping lights.

When I visited church as a seeker, I was attracted by its use of visual images. Back then, this was mostly multi-media, where several slide projectors were used to flash images that blended with each other to create a dynamic effect. In fact, the church was spending a disproportionate amount of its income in producing a short multi-media piece for each service because they were so powerful in connecting with Unchurched Harry and Mary.

I remember one multi-media production that featured two

clay figures—one a grandfatherly God; the other, a man who was trying to please Him. The sound track was the man's earnest but garbled voice as he pondered how to make God happy. He offered God his money, his hobbies, his house—he even offered to march around with a sign that said, "Repent." But God wasn't interested. At the end, the man realized that what God really wanted was his heart, and when he offered it, God pulled him onto His lap and embraced him.

There I sat, a street-toughened newspaperman, and I had tears in my eyes! Those goofy little clay figures had succeeded in doing an end-run around my emotional defense system.

Multi-media can be used in a variety of effective ways. Beautiful images of nature, with majestic music as a background, can be used to open people's eyes to God's creative work. Or people on the street can be interviewed about who they think Jesus is, and a media could show slides of them while their opinions are aired. Or the theme of a song can be illustrated with a variety of photographs while it's played. While they're time-consuming to produce, multi-media productions can elicit a big payback.

As video has become less expensive, churches have started exploring that medium as well. For instance, the showing of short interviews with people or even scenes from motion pictures can be effective. Once in the middle of a message on hope, I stopped to show a scene from the popular movie *City Slickers*, where the characters were talking about getting a "do over" in life. The scene amplified my point that God offers "do overs" to all of us.

As I mentioned earlier, I presented two messages called "The Case for Christ" in which I used a courtroom-style approach to establish that Jesus is God. But instead of my reciting the historical evidence for the deity of Christ, I interspersed video snippets of scholars whom I had interviewed earlier. They became the "witnesses" in the "trial," boosting the credibility of the information in the eyes of skeptics.

• Reason #4: They didn't use art to preach.

Art deals best with emotions, not solutions. It's better at raising questions than providing answers. When churches try to preach with art, it comes off as didactic, but when they use it to lower defenses, identify with emotions, and raise issues, it can be extremely potent.

Drama provides a good illustration. For instance, if you're going to deal with the topic of unanswered prayer, sometimes the temptation is to present a drama that tries to teach a lesson, drive home a biblical principle, or show characters who neatly resolve their problem, as in a TV sitcom. But that would ring hollow to Unchurched Harry and Mary, who are demanding more sophisticated and detailed answers than can be presented through a brief, broad-brush dramatic scene.

But if the drama peeks into the lives of people who are frustrated by unanswered prayer and lets the audience identify with the intensity of their feelings, this will open up the issue for Harry and Mary and keep them riveted on the speaker who follows.

I've seen one drama on this topic where a couple is just about to adopt a child after years of prayerful and painful waiting, but the mother decides at the last moment to keep her baby. The scene ends with the couple's hugging in tears, not knowing which way to turn, wondering why God has apparently turned a deaf ear to their fervent prayers all those years. Nearly everyone in the audience can relate to that because all of us, to one degree or another, have wondered why God hasn't given us what we've asked for.

In effect, this drama says, *We're not out of touch. We understand the suffering you've gone through; we're aware of the hurt you've experienced. It's okay to feel those emotions. But now, let's allow the speaker to give us some biblical wisdom on how to understand this issue.*

As one drama writer, Judson Poling, told me, "The drama's

job is just to open up a can of worms and sort of stick our fingers in there and stir them around. Then it's the speaker's job to deal with the worms."

• **Reason #5: They made me laugh.**

The last thing I ever expected to do at a church service was to laugh. I expected to get angry, bored, or sleepy—but laugh? No way!

Yet there were plenty of times when I was attending church as a seeker that I ended up laughing hysterically at a sketch that was as clever as anything on "Saturday Night Live." Appropriate humor is important in dealing with seekers because:

• It's unexpected, so it disarms them.

• It dismantles their stereotypes of church.

• It shows that people in the church are "normal" and enjoy having a good time.

• It shows them that while Christianity is serious, we don't have to take ourselves too seriously. In other words, it's not a prerequisite to Christianity that a person be a stuffed shirt.

• It establishes common ground. After all, usually we laugh at humorous things because we can personally identify with the situation being presented.

• It breaks down defenses; when they laugh, people are more receptive to new ideas.

For years I had heard the psychological principle that laughter opens up people to different opinions, but I saw it for myself not long ago when I was watching a TV show. Though the program was endorsing behavior that I certainly didn't agree with, the humor had me laughing so hard that I was actually feeling positive toward what was being promoted. Finally I had to stop myself and say, *Wait a second—this is just propaganda! I don't believe this stuff!* My laughter had lowered my defenses enough so that ideas I didn't agree with were starting to gain a foothold.

I'm not saying we should use humor to try to brainwash

people into the kingdom. However, we have to recognize that for a variety of reasons, Unchurched Harry and Mary come into church wearing invisible armor to protect themselves, and I believe that God can use humor to penetrate their defenses.

CREATING A CREATIVE PROGRAM

You can make a difference in developing services and events that will creatively communicate to Unchurched Harry and Mary. Whether it's by developing your own creative gifts, encouraging others who have untapped talents, or taking part in brain-storming sessions on how the creative dial can be turned up, you have a role to play.

You might be an elder, a deacon, a Sunday school teacher, an usher, or a custodian at your church. Regardless of your involvement, you can increase the creativity when you begin asking yourself: *How can we do old things in new ways that will connect better with Unchurched Harry and Mary?*

That requires prayer, research to determine what appeals to the target audience, and plenty of planning. It helps to visit other churches as well as secular venues to see what kinds of creative concepts they're experimenting with.

In the case of seeker-targeted services, there needs to be advance coordination with the speaker because every aspect of the program—music, drama, multi-media, readings, dance, or video—should be centered as much as possible on the same theme. For each element of the program, ask yourself, *What can we do to communicate better?*

For instance, let's look at just one element of a service. Most churches devote a few minutes to having someone read Scripture. But instead of merely reading some verses, why not have the person reflect on the passage during the week so that he can tell a personal anecdote that relates to the verses before he reads them? This can be helpful in illustrating the practical application of that passage in a person's life and also whet the audience's appetite for the upcoming message.

Or perhaps props could be used, since the more senses that can be engaged in the listener, the longer he will retain the information. Once the climax to an anecdote I was telling was the fact that snow had started to fall. But rather than me just saying it snowed, at the right moment it actually began to "snow" on the stage behind me. People went home and told their friends, "You'll never guess what happened in church today. It snowed!" Maybe that piqued their curiosity enough that they might check out the church themselves. Occasionally I have used sound effects—like thunder rumbling, or glass breaking—to drive home a point.

Instead of having just one person read a passage, sometimes churches have several people go back and forth as they read numerous verses that relate to the topic of the day. For example, hearing people read twenty Bible verses on the topic of forgiveness or God's love can be a powerful presentation.

Some churches project the day's Scripture onto a screen while it's being read or have it printed in the program so that seekers aren't fumbling through a Bible to find it. From time to time, I've compiled verses on the day's topic and made copies available for people as they leave so they could take them home to reflect on them. That's a big help for Unchurched Harry and Mary, who are untrained in finding verses on a theme. It also puts Scripture in their hands and makes it accessible to them during the week.

Or one of the easiest ways to add variety is to have someone read a passage from a Christian book and then relate it to a specific passage of Scripture. Selections from writers like Max Lucado, or Ken Gire, or Chuck Swindoll can give the audience fresh insights into biblical truth.

There's no end to the possibilities when the status quo starts to get questioned and we unleash our God-given gifts. Unchurched Harry and Mary are saying, "Gimme creativity"— and as the Harvard student observed, it won't even take a lot for us to blow 'em away.

13

"GIMME SOMETHING GOOD"

My friend Trevor Waldock was an irreligious teenager when someone brought him to an evangelistic event held in a barn near his home in England. By the end of the evening, Trevor had committed his life to Christ, and ever since then he has been passionate about bringing the Gospel to Britain's "Unchurched Nigel and Rhoda."

That's a daunting challenge because British society is heavily secularized, with only ten percent of the population attending church each week compared to about forty percent in the U.S.[1]

Between the spring and fall of 1991, Trevor and some friends coalesced fifty-five Christians around the idea of forming a church where they could bring their unchurched friends. Together, they launched the Waterfront Church on January 5, 1992, meeting in a hotel in Southampton.

But the attendance at their first seeker service baffled Trevor. While he was pleased that eighty people showed up, which is more people than attend the average British church,[2] he couldn't understand why members of his core group hadn't invited more of their friends to their inaugural service.

He soon got his answer. The following week, attendance jumped to about 120 people, and suddenly Trevor realized what had happened.

"Our core people had to see firsthand the kind of service we were actually going to do so that they would have enough confidence to bring their unchurched friends," he said later. "Once they saw the excellence level was high enough, they were more willing to go out and invite people to the second service."[3]

It was a powerful lesson on the importance of excellence in any event or service geared to the unchurched. While Trevor's ministry lacked the financial resources of many established churches, its members made sure that whatever they presented was done with quality and concern for detail. As a result, the Christians who invited their friends didn't experience what another friend, John Lewis, calls "the cringe factor."

He's referring to what happens when a Christian finally gets up enough nerve to invite his unbelieving friend to church, and the Christian quietly cringes through the service because of the off-key singing, out-of-tune piano, bad acoustics, malfunctioning microphones, and disjointed sermon.

He's cringing because he realizes that the church's atmosphere is subtly saying to his friend, "This is a place where halfhearted efforts are good enough, because, frankly, we don't care enough to appropriately honor God or our guests."

QUALITY COUNTS

The cringe factor is a major reason why many church members turn a deaf ear when pastors plead for them to invite Unchurched Harry and Mary to a service or event. You see, they don't want to subject themselves or anyone else to the anxiety and embarrassment that are generated when a program is poorly produced.

Unfortunately, while the secular world is pursuing excellence in business and industry, many ministries are mired in mediocrity, and that's a major stumbling block to reaching the unchurched. In sum, "good enough" just isn't good enough in trying to reach seekers.

After all, it's biblical for God's people to honor God with the best that they have. Under the Old Testament's sacrificial system, it was unblemished lambs that were supposed to be offered to Him.[4]

It's important to emphasize that the pursuit of excellence doesn't mean neurotic perfectionism. Yet it does mean that the building, grounds, sanctuary, music, drama, media, and message are the best that can be accomplished given the church's level of resources and talents.

I've been at churches where paint was peeling from the walls, sound systems were plagued by distortion, lighting was so dim I could barely see the face of the speaker, musicians read their lyrics instead of having them memorized, and the message sounded as if it were ad-libbed.

Church members seemed oblivious to their surroundings because that's how church has always been done. But if they could see the service through the eyes of an unchurched person who spends his weekdays pursuing excellence in his career, they'd experience the cringe factor for themselves.

When I first attended church at Leslie's invitation, the excellence with which ministry was pursued helped create a common bond with me. In my own life, I worked hard to be the best journalist I could be, and my attitude was far from unique. Go to any library and you'll see books titled, *Excellence in Banking*, *Excellence in Education*, *Excellence in Leadership*, *Excellence in Management*, *Excellence in the Public Sector*, and so on.

So when I saw a church where people were intent on

creating a well-planned, well-produced service and where they obviously cared as much about the outcome as I cared about the articles I wrote for the newspaper, I felt a connection with them.

The pursuit of excellence requires the planning of each aspect of the event or service with clear goals in mind, keeping an eye out for details, and anticipating the reaction of Unchurched Harry and Mary. Leaders also must be willing to make last-minute changes to eliminate a song that's marginal, or a drama that isn't quite coming together.

And there's no question about it: Pursuing excellence is going to ruffle some feathers among people who believe that what was done in the past for church folks is good enough for unchurched folks. But as Franky Schaeffer said in his book, *Addicted to Mediocrity*:

"The idea that 'the Spirit can work somehow,' that God can bring something out of it if we just sort of throw it out there, is unjustifiable from those who aim to know the living God and can see His integrity and dedication to quality in His Word and the world around us."[5]

Besides, Unchurched Harry and Mary are often looking for excuses to ignore the truth of Christianity. "We don't want anything to distract them from the central message," said Nancy Beach, who's in charge of programming at Willow Creek Community Church. "If a vocalist is off-key, or poorly prepared, or too frightened to look at the congregation, the message of the song will surely be lost."[6]

THE BENEFITS OF EXCELLENCE

Nancy Beach once told me about an unanticipated benefit of producing a seeker service with excellence. She described how a young couple in the church, both extremely gifted as musicians, stepped forward to offer their assistance after seeing the level of quality at the services. Today, they're key contributors to the church's program and have helped elevate the quality of the services to new heights.

The lesson that Nancy said she learned was that *excellence attracts excellence*. Conversely, a sloppy and uninspired service can deter talented people from volunteering to help because they're hesitant to get involved in a production that's going to embarrass themselves and their audience.

And there are other benefits, too. For instance, I know a woman who was a spiritual seeker and who tried several churches but was dissatisfied with the quality of their children's programs. The student-teacher ratio was poor and the teachers seemed intolerant of her son, who was somewhat hyperactive. She was about to give up on church when a friend directed her to one in her area that was noted for its youth ministry.

Deciding to give church one last chance, she took her son there and stayed with him during the service to see how the children were treated. She was impressed by how capable, caring, and creative the volunteers were.

After a few weeks of staying in her son's class, she was comfortable enough to venture into the adult service. Not only did she end up giving her life to Christ at one of those services, but several months later her husband followed suit.

And guess where they serve today? In that church's Sunday school class, building into children for the benefit of both the kids *and* their parents.

ACHIEVING EXCELLENCE

Excellence doesn't have to be elusive. It begins with a mindset that God demonstrated excellence when He created the world and declared it to be "very good,"[7] and likewise we should maximize the abilities He has given us to create the best possible programs to proclaim His message. Here are some suggestions for helping ensure quality in whatever event you do for seekers:

• **Start with well-defined goals.**

The overall quality of a program is going to depend largely on whether all participants are aiming at the same target. A clear up-front understanding of what you're trying to accomplish will help in weeding out extraneous material and in selecting appropriate elements.

For instance, some friends and I once put together a breakfast to try to reach men who were reluctant to take the step of attending a regular church service. We wanted our event to be pre-evangelistic; that is, our main goal was to get Unchurched Harry inside the church to gain his trust and so he could see that we were normal people. That way, he might become willing to attend a more overtly evangelistic service at a later time.

With that objective in mind, we focused on developing a program to hit our target. We arranged for a well-known Chicago sportscaster to be our speaker because men always seem to be interested in behind-the-scenes anecdotes about the local teams and athletes. We coached him in weaving the story of his Christian faith into his presentation in a low-key way.

Since laughter bonds people and lowers defenses, we showed a video of sports "bloopers" on a projection TV during breakfast. Owing to a limited budget, we kept the meal and decorations simple so that we could concentrate on maintaining quality. And to make sure that Unchurched Harrys actually attended, we only sold tickets in pairs and told each Christian he was required to bring at least one unbeliever.

The event exceeded our expectations. I remember one woman's saying later, "My husband always said he'd never go to a church service, but he came to the breakfast and said to me afterward, 'These guys are all right; how about if we go to a service Sunday morning?' Can you believe that? I've been inviting him to church for years and he's been turning me down, and now *he* suggests it!"

What set us on the course toward quality and success was

the up-front decision to clearly define and articulate the purpose of the program so that every element worked toward the same objective. What's more, having concrete goals helped us to better evaluate the event after it was over.

• **Serve out of giftedness.**

In the spiritual gifts that God has implanted in each of His followers, He has collectively given us the raw material we need to reach out to seekers in a quality way. And when we yield those gifts to His service and allow the Holy Spirit to energize them, that's when there's potential for having a great impact in evangelism.

It makes sense that the best teaching comes from people with teaching gifts, the most inspired leadership comes from those gifted in leadership, and the most powerful music and acting comes from those who have gifts of creative communication. Our task, then, should be to discover what our gifts are, affirm them in each other, learn how to develop them, and then search out appropriate ways to express them.

One challenge is to separate the "want-to"s from the "able-to"s. The "want-to"s are those who have a desire to act in a drama or sing a song at a seeker event, but they lack the requisite spiritual gift and consequently they're only capable of achieving limited degrees of excellence. The "able-to"s are those who possess the necessary gift and who therefore have great potential for performing with quality if they open themselves to the Holy Spirit.

When Christians are operating in community, where they're secure in their love for each other, it's much easier to gently direct the "want-to"s away from inappropriate places of service and into the arena where they can make a quality contribution. Sometimes this can be difficult, but there's too much at stake to let the excellence of a seeker event be compromised, or to rob a person of the joy he would experience if he were serving in his gift area.

Few things are as exciting or humbling as watching the Holy Spirit activate someone's spiritual gift and elevate the excellence level beyond what the person could attain in his own strength.

I remember speaking at a seeker event and feeling that if I were a baseball player, my talk would have been the equivalent of a high fly ball that should have been easily caught by the centerfielder for the final out. But instead, it was as if the wind of the Holy Spirit blew the ball out of the park for a home run. All I could do was watch the results in awe because I knew that I certainly hadn't hit the ball that hard.

I can see the difference between someone who is merely able to carry a tune and another person whose spiritual gift enables him to sing a song that penetrates callous hearts. I've seen people who have a divine enablement to work with their hands in a way that gives them an edge in excellence.

The Body of Christ—His church, with each component part contributing to the whole—is an astounding organism that operates with excellence when we encourage it to function the way that God intended.

• **Speed of the leader, speed of the team.**

People take cues from leaders. That puts a special responsibility on those in leadership to establish through their own example that they're concerned about quality.

When I attended church as a seeker, I remember seeing the senior pastor walk across the lobby one day and bend down to pick up a tiny piece of paper. That sent a message to me: He must care about visitors because he obviously is concerned about the environment he's inviting them into. And he was sending an important message to every volunteer by illustrating that everybody must do his or her part in assuring quality.

Regardless of your own level of involvement at church, your personal commitment to making your contribution with excellence will be an encouragement to others to do the same.

• **Details make a difference.**

In the mid-1980s, a chain of movie theaters in England was planning to launch an innovative advertising campaign to lure people away from their TVs and videotape recorders.

"Once a style of advertising had been agreed on, it dawned on someone that people might turn up at the movie theater, see frayed carpet, be greeted by rude, gum-chewing ushers, and perch on broken seats while sitting cross-legged to avoid visiting the foul-smelling washrooms. Things had to change. Uniforms were introduced, staff re-trained, and building and furnishings upgraded. The advertising worked, people enjoyed their night out, and movie theater attendance in the U.K. continues to increase."[8]

The moral: Before you invite guests over, first clean the house. Not only should a church program be done with quality to avoid the cringe factor, but everything from the condition of the carpet to the painting of the walls should be examined with fresh eyes to make sure that they send the message that visitors matter.

One denomination, in encouraging its churches to experiment with seeker events, actually issued a checklist to help them do a detailed quality assessment.

"Do your buildings put people off?" the material asked. "Does the outside need a new bulletin board, painting, litter cleared, grounds tidied, basic repairs? And what about the inside? Could the welcome be enhanced by improving the heating, washroom facilities, decor, entrance area, furnishings, direction signs, bulletin boards, and books? In all of these areas we are trying to remove the unnecessary barriers that stand in the way of people becoming part of the church family."[9]

• **Do only what you can do well.**

I know of one church whose music ministry was weak because it was going through a transition. So instead of doing three mediocre songs during their seeker service, they chose to do only one per week but to do it with compelling quality. As a result of the excellence with which it was performed, people were deeply moved by that single song. Rather than doing other music, the church got creative by renting and showing some high-quality video and multi-media productions and had someone read relevant selections from Christian books.

Sometimes churches get the idea that if it's a good idea to have one song, it's a better idea to have three; if it's a good idea to do a drama twice a month, it's a better idea to do one weekly. But quality declines when quantity is pushed too far. Given a choice, sacrifice quantity for quality.

• Do the hard work.

Regardless of giftedness, excellence requires hard work. I know one talented teacher who spends thirty hours per week writing his Sunday message because that's what it takes for him to move beyond "acceptable" to "excellent." Another friend of mine spends eight hours researching, writing, and memorizing a six-minute talk he gives during the Scripture time at a seeker service.

I know of a volunteer—in fact, he's the owner of his own successful business—who spends his Saturday mornings scrubbing his church's windows until they sparkle. I know volunteers at a church meeting in a movie theater who get up before the sun on Sundays to clean up the stray kernels of popcorn and sticky gum that the theater's own cleaning crew missed the night before.

There is no shortcut to consistent quality. Excellence requires an investment of time and effort. People who are concerned about quality set the right priorities to free up adequate time because they understand that going the extra mile can have a big payoff for seekers.

• Know unchurched people.

Understanding your target audience—not just in an abstract, statistical way but through a face-to-face relationship—is vital in knowing how to produce an event with excellence. It causes a person to think in advance, "If I were to invite my neighbor Jim to this program, how would he respond?" Or, "If Nancy from work invested an hour of her time in attending this event, would she feel ripped off?" Or, "If my brother-in-law attended this service, would he want to come back for another one, or will he make an excuse the next time I invite him?"

And after the event, ask your unchurched friends for their assessment of the experience. Specifically, what attracted them and what distracted them? Not only will you gather helpful research for planning future events, but merely soliciting their feedback communicates that their opinions are valued.

• Sacred cows produce stale churches.

Evaluation is critically important in guarding against the entropy that can erode a church's level of quality. But evaluation is only effective when it's prompt, specific, honest, reciprocal, and complete. That means the elimination of sacred cows that have been exempt from scrutiny in the past.

For instance, at some churches the pastor's message is the only element of the service that's off limits for post-event analysis. That kind of dual standard can produce simmering resentment among others whose contributions are fair game for evaluation.

Immediately after I speak at a seeker service or event, I receive written feedback from discerning leaders in the church. Often, it's affirming, but many times there will be some tactful suggestions for improvement. I try to remain receptive to any input where the person is speaking the truth in love. In fact, looking back over the years, it's clear that any improvement in my speaking has largely been a product of the honest evaluation of others.

ANTICIPATING EXCELLENCE

More than a decade ago, Thomas J. Peters and Robert H. Waterman, Jr. analyzed the best-run corporations in the country and distilled the lessons they learned into a trend-setting book called *In Search of Excellence*.[10] They emphasized the need to respect the dignity of people, the necessity of maintaining simplicity, and the important role of constantly monitoring the level of quality to guard against erosion.

Their landmark book helped shape the increasing American expectation of excellence—an expectation that will color the way Unchurched Harry and Mary react to your efforts to reach them with the Gospel.

"Gimme something good," they're saying. Because when we don't, we're saying back to them, "You don't matter enough to me to do my best."

14

"GIMME SOMETHING FROM THE HEART"

When I walked into church as a skeptical unbeliever, my "hypocrisy antenna" was scanning the place for signs that people were just playing church. In fact, I was aggressively on the lookout for phoniness, opportunism, or deception, because I felt that if I could find an excuse for rejecting the church on grounds of hypocrisy, I could feel free to reject Christianity as well.

But what I found amazed me: *These people really believed this stuff.* I didn't agree with them, but I couldn't dismiss their sincerity and conviction.

Someone once said that the biggest obstacle to reaching the unchurched is unconverted clergy. As a reporter I had met my share of slick ministers who were running more of a scam than a ministry. On top of that, I knew plenty of people who would claim to be Christians if you pressed them about it, but you'd never know it by the lives they were living.

Yet that didn't seem to be the fuel that this church was running on. I came away convinced that they honestly believed there's a real heaven and a real hell and that people's eternities are hanging in the balance. That's something you can't fake. If you try, Unchurched Harry and Mary will call you on it sooner or later.

After all, many Unchurched Harrys and Marys are already cynical about Christianity. When people were asked in a national survey to rank professions for honesty and integrity, they placed TV evangelists near the bottom of seventy-three occupations, right between prostitutes and organized crime bosses.[1]

The degree of hostility could be seen when lawyers tried to select a jury to hear a lawsuit against a TV minister in the fall of 1992. The potential jurors "expressed such deep resentment toward television evangelists that an impartial, twelve-person jury could not be selected. When asked if they could set aside their feelings to decide the case on its merits, one potential juror after another said no. 'It's a giant rip-off,' said one. 'I think they're thieves,' said another."[2]

Organized religion's image also has been tarnished by allegations of sexual misconduct by clergy. In the last decade, four hundred priests have been accused in criminal or civil cases of sexual abuse.[3] In October 1992, the news media gave extensive coverage to three hundred abuse victims and their relatives who banded together to form a support organization and hold a convention near Chicago.[4]

These developments, plus the trend toward more skepticism of institutions in general, make many unchurched people wary about the faith. In fact, for quite a few, it was hypocrisy that steered them away from church in the first place.

Two famous examples are Gandhi, who spurned Christianity partly because of his encounters with mean-spirited people who claimed they were Christians, and Karl Marx, who became deeply disillusioned after his father suddenly abandoned his once deeply held faith and began attending the Lutheran church merely to make more contacts for his business.[5]

That's why authenticity in individual Christians and within the local church is so critically important in reaching Unchurched Harry and Mary. They want to see integrity in the way Christians treat each other, deal with people outside the church, and live out their faith in the world.

BLENDING BELIEF AND BEHAVIOR

Of course, integrity can be a slippery word to define. It's like the story of some theologians who were trying to come up with an accurate definition of the word, so they invited a philosopher into the room. "Tell us," they said, "what is integrity?"

The philosopher pondered the question. "Integrity," he finally intoned, "is what you're like when nobody's around."

The panel thanked him, then ushered in a businessman and asked for his definition. "In my world," the businessman said, "integrity means a person is as good as his word."

After thanking him, the panel invited a lawyer to join them. "What is integrity?" they asked.

The attorney's eyes cautiously scanned the room. He crept over to the door, opened it, looked outside to make sure nobody was listening, and then bolted it shut. He closed the windows and pulled down the shades.

"Tell me," he finally whispered, "what do you *want* it to mean?"

But Unchurched Harry and Mary know instinctively what integrity means. To them, having integrity means there's an integration between a person's beliefs and behavior. In fact, Warren Wiersbe points out that the word "integrity" comes from the root word *integer*, meaning "wholeness" and "intact." Wiersbe adds:

"Integrity is to personal or corporate character what health is to the body or 20/20 vision is to the eyes. A person with integrity is not divided (that's *duplicity*) or merely pretending (that's *hypocrisy*). He or she is 'whole;' life is 'put together,' and things are working together harmoniously. People with integrity have nothing to hide and nothing to fear. Their lives are open books."[6]

A FAITH THAT TRANSFORMS

That's what integrity is: a combination of creed and character. Unfortunately, a researcher has concluded that only about thirteen percent of Americans have what can be called "transforming faith," through which their professed beliefs make a consistent, day-to-day difference in their life.[7]

In other words, where they don't just say they believe in the dignity of life, but it shows in the way they treat the needy and disadvantaged. They don't just believe the Bible is God's revelation to the world, but they study and apply it. They don't just believe that God wants a relationship with them, but they consistently relate to Him in prayer.

They don't just think that it's a good idea for their children to learn about God, but they actively coach them in learning about God. They don't just believe that the church is a community of God's people, but they participate on a regular basis. Their spiritual outlook influences every dimension of their life, including the way they do business, treat their spouse, and handle conflict.

That impresses Unchurched Harry and Mary. But what distresses them is when they see people living a life that's sort of like my pet chinchilla's. You see, because our family has allergies to dogs and cats, a few years ago we bought a chinchilla, which looks like a cross between a squirrel and a rabbit. Because they're very curious animals, chinchillas need mental stimulation. So each evening my son, Kyle, opens Dusty's cage and lets him explore part of the house, and then after a while he snaps his fingers and Dusty scrambles back inside.

That's like the faith that many people have. They keep their Christianity caged up inside of them during the week so that it won't roam free and influence their lifestyle. Then on Sunday morning, they open the cage and let out their faith for an hour or so, always being careful to lock it back up before they drive home at the end of the service.

When Unchurched Harry and Mary detect that kind of superficial spirituality, their hypocrisy alarm goes off. Few things repel them as much as people who claim that Christ is the most important person in their life, and yet whose daily pattern of living gives away the fact that they are barely acquainted with Him.

However, when they see a person living out his faith in an authentic way, it can provide a powerful pull toward Christ. That's what Glenn Heck found out.

Though he was raised in a Christian family, Glenn's faith went on the rocks during his college days in the 1940s when he began doubting its intellectual underpinnings. He was becoming increasingly convinced that Christianity was a myth—until he encountered some students who were living out their Christian commitment with integrity.

Glenn's roommate, Rollin Reasoner, unknowingly played a pivotal role in reawakening Glenn's faith. According to an account of Glenn's experience:

Rollin was determined to pursue his personal devotions without flaunting them before his doubting roommate. So, every winter morning at 3:00 A.M., as Glenn slept with the window open, Rollin donned two overcoats and sat at his desk in fellowship with Christ.

"He sat there quietly singing, 'Jesus, I am resting, resting, in the joy of what Thou art,'" Glenn recalls. "As I watched that night after night, I finally came to the conclusion that you don't 'phony up' Christianity at 3:00 A.M. in a freezing room."

It was a turning point that brought Glenn back to an open and confident faith in the truth of Christianity.[8]

THE BOTTOM LINE: HONESTY

Unchurched people aren't looking for perfection in Christians, just honesty. They don't want them to pretend their lives are problem-free; they merely want an admission that they struggle, too. It's when Unchurched Harry and Mary see a collection of Christians hiding behind a facade of perfection that they begin to smell a cover-up.

William J. Murray recounts the story of a state official in Missouri who made front-page news when he was arrested for shoplifting a bottle of wine at a supermarket and then drank it while hiding in the store's restroom. Asked why he did it, he told police: "I'm a Southern Baptist deacon, and Southern Baptist deacons don't buy wine."

For years, this man had kept his drinking problem a secret, even from his closest church friends. The reason? "I felt," he said, "that I should not have faults."[9]

The Bible says we all have faults.[10] What makes Christians different is that we've been forgiven and are seeking, with God's help, to live changed lives. "There is no slander in the charge that the church is full of sinners," R. C. Sproul said. "Such a statement would only compliment the church for fulfilling her divinely appointed task."[11]

Conceding that we're sinners is a sign of integrity to Unchurched Harry and Mary. Frankly, they're repulsed by the pious deception of pretending that the Christian life is free of temptations, difficulties, and failures.

THE BUCK STOPS HERE

For many non-Christians, the test of whether a church has integrity is based on how it deals with financial matters. Crassly put, Unchurched Harry and Mary are demanding to know: *Are you motivated by your heart or your wallet?*

There's no shortage of statistics to demonstrate their concern about how finances are handled. For example, when George Gallup, Jr., conducted a wide-ranging national survey on religion, he found that "too much concern for money" was the Number One reason given by people for why they have abandoned church, being mentioned by nearly four out of ten unchurched individuals.[12]

Pollster George Barna interviewed a random cross-section of 906 unchurched adults and found that fifty-one percent believe that churches are "too concerned about raising money."[13]

When I first went to church, I suspected that the ministry's real goal was to fleece me. Actually, I was secretly hoping I would find the church was a scam because not only would I have a front-page story for *The Chicago Tribune*, but I could reject the church and its God along with it. But, bit by bit, the church dismantled my skepticism.

For instance, newcomers were invited not to contribute to the church. At the time the offering was received, someone would say, "If you're visiting with us today, we're glad to have you as our guest. Please don't feel any obligation to participate in this part of the service. In fact, we hope you'll consider this service our gift to you. This offering is an opportunity for those of us who are regular attenders to invest tangibly in what God is doing here."

There were no fund-raising thermometers on the walls, no pledge system, no bingo games or car washes, no gimmicks or high-pressure tactics. The Christians supported the ministry financially because they had been taught that this is how God underwrites His work in the local church. By exempting visitors from the expectation of giving, the church was sending them a signal that said, *Our agenda is to help you, not to help ourselves.*

A MATTER OF MOTIVES

At one point, I thought I had figured out the church's ploy. Walking through the lobby after a service, I saw a booth where cassette tapes of the message were available. "Aha!" I said to myself. "Now I get it. The pastor gives a compelling and inspiring talk, and then they soak you for a tape of it. Everybody knows there's big profit in audio cassettes. That's how they cash in!"

So I went over to the booth. "How much are you selling those tapes for?" I asked the woman behind the counter.

"One dollar, eighty-seven cents, plus tax," she said.

"Oh," I replied, disappointed that I hadn't uncovered their angle. After all, a blank tape nearly costs that much!

"But," she added quickly, "if you can't afford that, you can just have one. Here, do you want to take one along? Let me just give you one."

"No, thanks," I said as I turned to walk away. But then I thought of a follow-up question. "Let me ask this: What cut does the speaker get of the $1.87?"

"Nothing," she replied.

"Oh."

Those tapes legitimately could have been priced higher. But keeping the cost low helped reassure skeptics like me that the church wasn't motivated by money but by a genuine concern for people.

Churches can defuse skepticism by being up-front about their finances. For example, at our church if someone comes up to the visitors' center and asks questions about the church's expenditures, the volunteer immediately offers him a copy of the church's full financial statement, audited by an outside accounting firm.

Like many ministries, the church is a member of the Evangelical Council for Financial Accountability, which enforces standards for fiscal responsibility. The church's senior pastor has voluntarily frozen his salary at a reasonable amount, and a percentage of any books published by the church staff goes back to the church's treasury.

I'm not suggesting that all churches should take those same steps. However, they should be aware that Unchurched Harry and Mary are looking for any evidence that the church's motives are impure.

I was reminded of that when I went to talk to journalism students at a local high school. During a question-and-answer time, someone asked me why I left a successful newspaper career to work in a church. "More money, huh?" he said.

He and his classmates presumed that my decision must have been driven by economics. When I explained that my income was cut in half when I went into ministry, they were dumbfounded—and they were then more receptive when I explained the real reason why I changed careers.

Adults are like that, too. For some of them, their financial skepticism needs to be satisfied before they'll become willing to listen to the message that you or your church is disseminating.

I remember sitting in during an interview between a *TIME* magazine reporter and Bill Hybels. In preparation for an article about the church, she went down a checklist of the same questions that are on the minds of many seekers:

• What's your salary?
• Do you own a vacation home?
• What kind of car do you own?
• How much did you pay for your house?
• Do you own an airplane?
• Do you own a sailboat?
• Is your benefit package different from that of the other staff members?[14]

Those are just the questions I remember! Of course, her unstated question was this: Are you in this for the bucks?

While few churches attract such scrutiny by the news media, *it's critical that all churches understand that they are under scrutiny by Unchurched Harry and Mary.*

How finances are handled is a litmus test for many of them. When it's done openly, with accountability and integrity—that is, when there's an integration between biblical principles of stewardship and how the church handles its funds—then that removes an obstacle for them in considering the church's message.

All of this means that those in church leadership must make sure their priorities are right. "Ministry takes money, but we have to be careful that money doesn't start taking the ministry," Wiersbe said. "When that happens, ministry stops, and the organization turns into a religious business."[15]

15

"GIMME SOMETHING I CAN RELATE TO"

Have you ever watched the body language of a skeptic at a seeker-oriented event? Often while the speaker is walking toward the front, Unchurched Harry and Mary are slowly folding their arms across their chest, narrowing their eyes, and slouching back in their chairs.

Their signal is clear: *Go ahead, hit me with your best shot. My defenses are in full force; let's see if you can break through.*

That was my attitude the first time I ventured inside a service for spiritual seekers. Sure, the music, drama, and multi-media helped make me more receptive to spiritual ideas, but when the message came I still had some residual resistance.

I was anticipating a stern, humorless lecture or, worse yet, a scolding. I expected to emerge feeling guilty like when I went to church as a child. Besides, being a baby boomer, I wasn't very respectful of authority figures. My attitude was, *What could some hot-shot minister who's probably out of touch with the real world have to say that will mean anything to my life?*

But I was disarmed that first Sunday. I was taken aback by the style and substance of the message. Not only did the sermon interest and challenge me, but it succeeded in launching me on my spiritual journey.

A lot of unchurched people are just waiting for those kind of messages. In fact, when unchurched people were asked what could bring them into a church, the Number One response, given by nearly one out of five, was better messages.[1] But how can we encourage that to happen? What kind of communication is going to be most effective in connecting with Unchurched Harry and Mary?

I know what worked with me. In fact, I'll recount seven characteristics of the messages I heard when I was a seeker that kept me engaged and coming back until I received Christ. By the way, several of these points also may be helpful in guiding Christians as they discuss spiritual matters in individual conversations with unbelievers.

• **Reason #1: The titles were intriguing.**

This sounds trivial, but it isn't. Before every service I was going to attend, I wanted to know the specific title and topic of the message. And I wasn't alone. A survey showed that 54% of unchurched people are "very" or "somewhat" interested in knowing the sermon title in advance.[2] The reason, of course, is that time is a precious commodity to Unchurched Harry and Mary, and they don't want to waste any of it by listening to a message on an irrelevant subject.

I'm not suggesting that churches give their sermons cute names, although I came close to crossing the line when I did a take-off on the movie title *Honey, I Shrunk the Kids* by calling a message "Honey, I Shrunk Our God." But the title should be intriguing enough to assure the skeptic that he'll reap dividends from his investment of time.

Some of Bill Hybels' titles that I've liked over the years at our church are "Fanning the Flames of Marriage" (even atheists want a better relationship with their spouse), "Turning Houses into Homes" (unbelievers want close families as much as Christians do), "Faith Has Its Reasons" (an intriguing concept to skeptics), and "God Has Feelings, Too" (a new twist in thinking about God). I've done messages called "The Rewards of Spiritual Risk-Taking," "God's Outrageous Claims," "The God of the Second Chance," and "It's A Good Thing I'm Not God."

"Alternatives to Christianity" was another winner. "That was an A+ title, as long as we dealt fairly with the opposing points of view," Hybels said. "I could have called the series 'The Danger of the Cults' or 'Why Christianity Is the Only Sensible Religion,' but those titles would have attracted only people who were already convinced. From the very first words people hear about our message, we need to communicate, 'This is for you. This is something you'll want to hear.' "[3]

When I did a series of messages on evolution and miracles, I called it "Believing the Unbelievable," because I wanted to connect with the attitude that skeptics had about those topics. When I tell the story of my spiritual journey at a seeker event, I call the talk "Surprised By God's Truth" in hopes that it will stimulate curiosity.

During the national flap over the pregnancy of a fictional unwed TV newswoman named Murphy Brown in 1992, I did a message called, "What Jesus Would Say to Murphy Brown." I followed that with, "What Jesus Would Say to Bart Simpson," referring to the trouble-prone cartoon character, and then one called, "What Jesus Would Say to Rob Sherman."

You may have never heard of Rob, but he's the most notorious atheist in Chicago and an acquaintance of mine. As national spokesman for American Atheists, Inc., he has stirred up many Christians by filing lawsuits over religious issues. Not only did that service attract a lot of unchurched people to see what

Jesus might say to a controversial person like Rob, but Rob even came and brought his family!

Hybels, who has mentored me in speaking to unchurched audiences, can spend hours trying to select appropriate titles for his messages. When I'm working on a series of my own, sometimes I'll give him a list of a dozen suggestions to get his feedback—and I'll get it back with *What else have you got?* scribbled across the top. He has urged me to spend the necessary time to come up with a compelling title because those ultimate consumers, Unchurched Harry and Mary, won't buy what doesn't interest them.

I hope you'll consider providing input for titles at your church. Some of the best ones I've heard have been suggested by people in the congregation. In fact, the Murphy Brown title was proposed at an annual message topic brain-storming session that's held with volunteers from our church.

Also, if you're teaching a Sunday school class or involved in the planning of any event, thinking through a title that will appeal to your target audience can go a long way in setting the proper tone for the program.

• Reason #2: The messages had high user-value.

My friends Mark and Heidi Mittelberg described to me how they spent a summer working with a London church, going door to door to invite people to visit a service. After several discouraging days of being turned down, one woman agreed to join them that Sunday.

Unfortunately, when they showed up for the service, the message topic happened to be, "Can A Christian Be Demon-Possessed?" Of course, their visitor found the subject odd and irrelevant. It was an unfortunate example of a church that had good evangelistic intentions but no place for Christians to take unbelievers where they could hear a message specifically tailored for their lives.

The most effective messages for seekers are those that

address their felt needs. Unchurched Harry and Mary want to know if a book that's centuries old can really give them practical assistance in the trenches of their daily lives.

They want to know if it can help them in dealing with their hurts, defusing their anger, resolving their conflicts, easing their fears, overcoming their loneliness, improving their parenting, fixing their relationships, understanding themselves, and generally coping with life. When messages address those issues head-on—and, equally important, when concrete application points are offered—seekers respond.

Here's what happened to me as a seeker. As I would listen to a series of messages on how to improve my marriage, I would conclude that the scriptural guidelines for marriage made sense. Of course, the reason they made sense is because they're from God. But even though I wasn't ready to accept that premise, I was still willing to try implementing the biblical principles simply because they sounded so reasonable. And when I began treating my wife in a biblical way, guess what happened? Our marriage improved!

As I began applying biblical wisdom to the way I dealt with my anger, I found my emotions getting under control. When I started practicing forgiveness the way the Bible prescribes, my bitterness eased. And as this happened again and again in areas of finances, relationships, and character qualities, it was building a case for the reliability of Scripture.

In other words, after a while I said to myself, "Maybe there *is* something to the Bible. When I try living the way it says I should live, my life gets better. Where did all that wisdom come from? Is it possible that the Bible really is a revelation from God?"

My ultimate conclusion that the Bible is God's inspired Word was the result not only of checking out its historical reliability but also of personally experiencing its ability to positively change my life, even though I wasn't yet a Christian.

So in talking to Unchurched Harry and Mary, consider

challenging them to do what King David suggested: "Taste and see that the Lord is good."[4]

• Reason #3: The messages dealt with the *why* as much as the *what*.

When I came to church, I viewed Christianity as a complex and restrictive set of rules that had been imposed in order to control people's lives. And, to be honest, I wasn't very interested in complying with any regulations that were going to hamper my rather free-wheeling lifestyle.

But what resonated with me was when a speaker wouldn't just say *what* God commanded but would explain *why* God took that stand. For instance, during my message on what Jesus would say to Murphy Brown, I could have gone down the list of God's commands about non-marital sex and tsk-tsked over the fact that Murphy had violated them.

But although I made it clear that she had, indeed, transgressed God's laws, I also talked extensively about why God gave us sexual boundaries in the first place. His motive wasn't to capriciously squelch our enjoyment of life but to lovingly protect us from harm because we matter so much to Him.

After all, He understands the emotional devastation that people can suffer when they get intimately involved with a person outside of the security of a marriage. He understands the loneliness that can result when intimacy is followed by abandonment. He understands the guilt and shame that can haunt people after sexual encounters that burn bright for a few moments but then turn cold. He understands the risks of sexually transmitted diseases. He understands that when pregnancy occurs, so often it's the father who takes off and it's the mother who is left with the grueling job of raising the child alone. And He understands that being reared in a one-parent family puts that child at risk in virtually every area of life—emotionally, intellectually, behaviorally, financially, and even physically.

That's one reason why God drew boundaries for our

sexuality—to save us from hurting ourselves. When communicators help Unchurched Harry and Mary understand that God's guidelines are motivated by His great love and concern for their well-being, He becomes a God they want to know more about.

• **Reason #4: The messages weren't holier-than-thou.**

Boy, I was ready and waiting for the pastor at that first seeker service to take a "holier-than-thou" approach in delivering his sermon. When a speaker exhibits that attitude, he becomes an easy target for a cynic such as I was.

Instead of listening to the message, I would have been sitting there mentally poking holes in him. "Sure, he comes off as this pious guy who thinks he has all the answers," I'd have been thinking. "But I'll bet he turns the air blue when his hammer slips and smashes his finger! I bet he kicks the dog just like everybody else does. Who's he trying to fool by trying to come off like Mr. Perfect?"

But this defense mechanism was short-circuited when the speaker poked holes in himself. I was amazed at how Bill Hybels would speak in very vulnerable terms about his own shortcomings and failures, about the areas of life in which he has struggled, and about the doubts he has wrestled with over the years. I couldn't knock him off his pedestal because he had never climbed onto one in the first place!

Unchurched people don't like to be talked down to. Sooner or later, they see through leaders who are trying to project a phony public image. They respond best when speakers talk to them as friends and peers, sharing with sincerity and honesty. They'll trade a polished performance for a straightforward talk any day.

I know some church leaders who feel that being transparent in their speaking would undermine their authority in the church. On the contrary, respect is earned when pastors stop pretending that they're above the struggles that everyone else deals with.

To Unchurched Harry and Mary, it's a credibility test.

They ask themselves, "Is this guy going to come clean about what his life is really like? Because if he isn't, why should I believe anything he's telling me?"

• Reason #5: The messages spoke my language.

My mental caricature of pastors was that they were academic bookworms who lived in ivory towers far removed from the real world. After all, many of them dressed differently, they graduated from special schools, they talked a different language, and they spent their time studying a book that was written in antiquity. I thought that if they were that insulated from the realities of my world, why should I listen to what they had to tell me?

At least, that was the stereotype I had until I began attending seeker services. There, I heard everyday language. When the speaker would pray, he wouldn't use a bunch of "thees" and "thous," but he would talk to God as if he actually knew Him.

When he would use stories to illustrate the points in his messages, he talked about riding his Harley-Davidson motorcycle, going sky-diving, or seeing a ball game. When he would quote an expert, it wasn't Augustine or Spurgeon but it was often people from outside the church's walls—people I knew about. And he would sprinkle in references to current events and controversies that people were talking about in coffee shops around town.

This communicated that he was an unpretentious guy who lives an active and interesting life, who has street smarts, and who was plugged into the same world as I was. In other words, he was the kind of person I'd like to get to know. And the fact that he was living a Christian life told me that it's possible for someone to integrate authentic faith into the real world.

He also was careful to define Christian terminology so that I didn't sit there feeling ignorant. In our increasingly secular society, fewer and fewer people come to church already understanding terms like "redemption" and "righteousness" or having even a rudimentary knowledge of biblical characters.

I was glad that when I first started attending church, Bill defined the word "grace." I used to think that grace was merely something that Christians would say before a meal. I thought "amazing grace" was a darn good prayer that someone said before a meal. Like, "That was amazing grace, Uncle Bob! Great job! Say that same prayer next Thanksgiving when we pray again."

There is, however, an ironic downside to translating Christianese into everyday words. Unchurched Harry and Mary appreciate it, but some Christians don't. Said Alan Walker:

"An idolatry of words has grown up in evangelism. There are many people who, if they fail to hear the repetition of phrases and words with which they are familiar, make the sometimes absurd claim that the Gospel is not being preached."[5]

Sometimes those kinds of unfair remarks are a price that has to be paid in order to connect meaningfully with irreligious people.

• Reason #6: The messages answered *my* questions.

Have you ever noticed that Christians are adept at answering the kind of questions posed by other Christians but inept at responding to the sort of inquiries that seekers want answered? So Christians end up debating the fine points of whether baptism ought to be by immersion or sprinkling and which eschatological interpretation is correct, while seekers are voting with their feet and heading away from church.

However, one thing that impressed me at the seeker services was that I heard messages that confronted tough issues. For example, the church did a series on prayer to help seekers understand what it means to communicate with their Creator, and one part was devoted to the question, "What about unanswered prayer?"

That's one of the biggest questions among unchurched

people on the topic of prayer, and the message didn't gloss over the issue or shortchange me with pat answers. Instead, the speaker delved into the heartbreak and frustration of feeling ignored by God and offered a sincere and well-reasoned response.

As a result, seekers didn't just learn about unanswered prayer; they also learned that Christians don't have to be afraid to discuss the more controversial aspects of their faith. That contributes greatly to credibility.

• Reason #7: The speaker actually seemed to like me.

For me, going into a church was like venturing behind enemy lines, and I figured people would feel the same way about my presence. I thought they were going to whisper behind my back, "Look! It's one of *them*. It's one of those hell-bound pagans! Quick, hide the valuables! Protect the women!"

But the environment of the church, and especially the attitude subtly expressed in the messages, was one of acceptance. I felt that the speaker actually cared about me. And he did. For Hybels, a prerequisite of effectively communicating to Un-churched Harry and Mary has always been that pastors *like* them:

"If we don't, it's going to bleed through our preaching. Listen closely to sermons on the radio or on television, and often you'll hear remarks about 'those worldly secular people.' Unin-tentionally, these speakers distance themselves from the non-Christian listener; it's us against them. I find myself wondering whether these preachers are convinced that lost people matter to God. It's not a merciful, 'Let's tell them we love them' but a ticked off, 'They're going to get what's coming to them!' These preachers forfeit their opportunity to speak to non-Christians because the unchurched person immediately senses, *They don't like me*."[6]

That's getting down to fundamentals, isn't it? The apostle Paul said, "If I speak in the tongues of men and of angels, but have not love, I am only a resounding gong or a clanging cymbal.

If I have the gift of prophecy and can fathom all mysteries and all knowledge, and if I have a faith that can move mountains, but have not love, I am nothing."[7]

Ultimately, if we aren't motivated to reach Unchurched Harry and Mary by our love for them, the results will be disheartening. When you don't really like unchurched people, you'll never get to know them well enough to relate to them in a meaningful way.

The flip side is that the more we care about them, the more we're going to naturally want to hang around them. And the more we get to know them, the more we'll be able to climb inside their minds. Then it becomes easier to determine how to best help them grasp the amazing reality that the age-old message of Christ is vitally relevant to their life in twentieth-century America.

16
STARTING YOUR EVANGELISTIC ADVENTURE

It was my birthday, and so I scheduled one of my favorite activities—having lunch with a spiritual skeptic.

He was a successful, street-wise building contractor whose daughter had started coming to our church. Although he was on the defensive as we started our conversation, soon he began asking insightful questions about Christianity.

As I laid out for him the biblical teaching on salvation, I could see a glimmer of understanding in his eyes. At the end, he said, "You know, I'm fifty-three years old, and nobody ever told me about grace before."

What was supposed to be an hour-long lunch stretched until four in the afternoon. By the time we shook hands at the end, he was clearly committed to sincerely seeking the truth about God, and I was reeling from the kind of fulfillment that's beyond my ability to describe.

What else could I have done that afternoon that would have been more important? Let's face it: no adventure is greater, no enterprise is more exciting, and no effort is more worthwhile than communicating Christ to irreligious individuals.

That's why I hope you'll finish this book not only with a better understanding of the minds of Unchurched Harry and Mary, but with a renewed commitment to reaching their hearts with the Gospel. I pray that you'll catch the vision of how your individual evangelistic efforts can be multiplied when you work in conjunction with your church to develop services, programs, and events that are *strategically* and *effectively* targeted to seekers.

I recently saw again the amazing way that these kind of partnerships can impact lives. I was planning to teach a four-week class for new Christians at our church, and I was going to devote the first week to a thorough recounting of the Gospel to make sure everyone in the class really was a Christian. So the preceding week, I mentioned at our seeker services that anyone who was curious about what it means to be a Christian would be welcome to attend that first session.

I don't know how many spiritual seekers were among the four hundred people who showed up for the class. However, I spent forty-five minutes meticulously going through the Gospel, and then I offered a prayer of repentance and salvation for those who were ready to put their trust in Christ. I asked all who had received Christ that evening to put an X on their class registration card so that I could identify them.

I knew that the Holy Spirit was up to something by the high attention level of the class and the way so many people greeted me afterward with tears in their eyes. As one Christian in the class told me later, "I sensed God was working on a lot of people, so when you were going through the Gospel, I just prayed the whole time."

Later we looked through the cards and found that eighty-eight people had committed their lives to Christ! Several cards had little notes, like, "Lee, I finally did it!" and, "Thanks for challenging me!"

I barely slept that night. My mind kept returning to the verse that says, "I tell you, there is rejoicing in the presence of the angels of God over one sinner who repents."[1]

Think of the great celestial celebration that evening!

To me, that incident was yet another confirmation of how a church's seeker-oriented approach can help individual Christians in their efforts to bring unbelievers into God's kingdom. Think through what had happened:

• Christians had built authentic friendships with these Unchurched Harrys and Marys and were praying fervently for the Holy Spirit to tenderize their hearts.

• The Christians had shared their faith as best they could and then invited their friend to attend one of our services designed for seekers.

• There, Unchurched Harry and Mary discovered a place that spoke their language and gave them the space they needed to check out Christianity at their own pace. They were intrigued enough to keep returning.

• As they heard about Christian principles for living, they undoubtedly tried some of them and found that they did improve their lives, giving credibility to the faith. They saw sincere people who enthusiastically invited questions about Christianity.

• Over time, I built up trust with them because I was one of the people who was often involved in these seeker services. They regarded me as someone who was shooting straight with them and not hiding behind a bunch of God-talk. So when I invited them to a class where they could take the next step toward investigating Christianity, many responded.

All I had to do at that point was to thoroughly explain the Gospel in terms they could understand and to take them by the hand as they stepped across the line of faith. For those who weren't ready yet, I encouraged them to continue using the church as a resource to get past whatever spiritual sticking point was hindering their progress.

That's kingdom teamwork! People praying, people building relationships with unbelievers, people using their spiritual gifts to create seeker-oriented services or events—it's a divine conspiracy to reach Unchurched Harry and Mary!

The question I want to conclude with is this: *Are you willing to be a conspirator?*

Are you willing to prioritize irreligious people in your life so that you have the time and inclination to develop meaningful relationships with them? And is your church willing to prioritize them—that is, to devote resources to create seeker-sensitive places where people can bring their unchurched friends?

Because you can count on this: *If Harry and Mary remain mere afterthoughts, the chances are they're also going to remain unchurched.*

You must be intentional in your efforts to reach them. You've just taken a step by reading this book so you can better understand their thinking, but unless this knowledge is translated into *specific* evangelistic action, it's a wasted effort.

Don't let yourself get overwhelmed by the size of the task. Jesus told His disciples to preach the Gospel to all nations, but to start where they were—right in Jerusalem.[2]

So start where you are. Think of three specific irreligious people in your own life—not a mass of faceless skeptics but three individuals within your sphere of influence. People you can pray for. People you can deepen your relationship with. People you can share your faith with over time. People you can invite to seeker-oriented events. Make them your personal mission field.

It's my hope that this book has given you some insights and inspiration to help you in this process. Please take seriously what I suggested in the first chapter—prayerfully consider the material in this book, take advantage of what's helpful, set aside the rest, and then embark on the next installment of your ongoing adventure of relational evangelism.

As you do that, keep in mind what King David wrote as he began the fortieth psalm. His words provide an apt ending for this book because they emphasize the incredible, undeserved work God has done *in* us—and the tremendous work He will do *through* us as we follow Him closely:

> I waited patiently for the Lord.
> He turned to me and heard my cry.
>
> He lifted me out of the pit of destruction,
> out of the sticky mud.
>
> He stood me on a rock
> and made my feet steady.
>
> He put a new song in my mouth,
> a song of praise to our God.
>
> Many people will see this and worship him.
> Then they will trust the Lord.[3]

ENDNOTES

CHAPTER 1

1. Sigmund Freud, *The Future of an Illusion* (New York: Norton, 1961), 30.

2. Joseph C. Aldrich, *Life-Style Evangelism* (Portland, Ore.: Multnomah, 1981), 19.

3. Romans 8:28

CHAPTER 3

1. Josh McDowell, *More Than a Carpenter* (Wheaton, Ill.: Living Books, 1977).

2. Josh McDowell, *Evidence That Demands a Verdict* (San Bernardino: Here's Life, 1979).

3. 2 Peter 1:16

4. 1 John 1:1

5. See Josh McDowell, *More Than a Carpenter*, 51–53, for a discussion of this topic.

6. Acts 2:22 (emphasis added)

7. Acts 2:32

8. Acts 2:41

9. 1 Corinthians 15:14

10. This point is discussed by Josh McDowell in *More Than a Carpenter*, 70–71.

11. John 20:28

12. Mark 14:61

13. See Mark 14:62

14. Mark 14:64

15. Josh McDowell, *Evidence That Demands a Verdict*, 62–63.

16. A. N. Sherwin-White, *Roman Society and Roman Law in the New Testament* (Grand Rapids, Mich.: Baker, 1978), 186–93.

17. See J. P. Moreland, *Scaling the Secular City* (Grand Rapids, Mich.: Baker, 1987), 150–51.

18. Josh McDowell, *Evidence That Demands a Verdict*, 166.

19. Peter W. Stoner, *Science Speaks* (Chicago: Moody Press, 1969), 107.

20. Ibid., 109.

21. Luke 24:44

22. Frank Morison, *Who Moved the Stone?* (Grand Rapids, Mich.: Lamplighter, 1958. Reprint of 1938 edition. London: Faber & Faber, Ltd.), 193.

23. Irwin H. Linton, *A Lawyer Examines the Bible* (Grand Rapids, Mich.: Baker, 1943), 36.

24. Simon Greenleaf, *An Examination of the Testimony of the Four Evangelists by the Rules of Evidence Administered in the Courts of Justice* (Jersey City, N.J.: Frederick D. Linn & Co., 1881).

25. See 1 Corinthians 15:6

26. Henry M. Morris, *The Bible and Modern Science* (Chicago: Moody, 1968), 95.

27. D. James Kennedy, *Why I Believe* (Dallas: Word, 1980), 33.

28. For a summary of evidence for Jesus outside the Bible, see Gary R. Habermas, *The Verdict of History: Conclusive Evidence for the Life of Jesus* (Nashville: Nelson, 1988).

29. Ezekiel 36:26

30. *National and International Religion Report*, October 19, 1992, 8.

31. Jeremiah 29:13

32. John 16:8

33. See Romans 3:11

34. James 5:16

CHAPTER 4

1. George Gallup, Jr., *The Unchurched American . . . 10 Years Later* (Princeton, N.J.: Princeton Religion Research Center, 1988), 2; George Gallup, Jr. and Jim Castelli, *The People's Religion: American Faith in the '90s* (New York: McMillan, 1989), 137–38; and George Barna, *Never On A Sunday* (Glendale, Calif.: Barna Research Group, 1990), 3–4. There is some variance in these findings and in how "unchurched" is defined. Gallup considers people unchurched if they aren't members of a church and haven't attended a service in the preceding six months, except for special religious holidays. Barna's definition is a person who has not attended a church worship service in a typical month.

2. Kenneth L. Woodward, et al., "Talking To God," *Newsweek*, January 6, 1992, 39.

3. James Patterson and Peter Kim, *The Day America Told the Truth* (New York: Prentice Hall, 1991), 201.

4. Kenneth L. Woodward, et al., "Talking To God," 39.

5. Ibid.

6. George Barna, *Never On A Sunday*, 3.

7. George Gallup, Jr., *The Unchurched American . . . 10 Years Later*, 30.

8. Ibid.

9. Hebrews 10:25

10. John R. W. Stott, *Basic Christianity* (Downers Grove, Ill.: InterVarsity Press, second edition, 1971), 7.

11. George Barna, *Never On A Sunday*, 3. Emphasis in original.

12. George Barna, *The Barna Report, 1992–1993* (Ventura, Calif.: Regal, 1992), 69.

13. Kenneth L. Woodward, et al., "Talking To God," 39.

14. James Patterson and Peter Kim, *The Day America Told the Truth*, 25.

15. Ibid., 200.

16. Ibid., 25–26.

17. George W. Cornell, "Situation Ethics Still Finding Favor," *The Arlington Heights (Ill.) Daily Herald*, May 23, 1992, sec. 5, 4.

18. Associated Press dispatch, "Church Lacks Hold Over Baby Boomers," *The Chicago Tribune*, June 5, 1992, sec. 2, 7.

19. Gary L. Collins and Timothy E. Clinton, *Baby Boomer Blues* (Dallas: Word, 1992), 39.

20. George Barna, *The Church Today* (Glendale, Calif.: Barna Research Group, 1990), 29.

21. "Did They Know Why They Were Celebrating Easter?" *Emerging Trends*, April 1991, 5.

22. George Barna, *The Frog in the Kettle* (Ventura, Calif.: Regal, 1990), 41.

23. Phillip L. Berman, *The Search For Meaning* (New York: Ballantine, 1990), 188.

24. Martin Robinson, *A World Apart* (Turnbridge Wells, England: Monarch, 1992), 99.

25. Gary R. Collins and Timothy E. Clinton, *Baby Boomer Blues*, 93.

26. Drew Kampion and Phil Catalfo, "All In The Family: What Do You Tell Your Children About Faith, Spirit, And The Meaning Of Life," *New Age Journal*, July/August 1992, 56.

27. See Douglas Groothuis, "That's Your Truth, I've Got My Own," *Moody Monthly*, March 1988, 21.

28. Phillip L. Berman, *The Search for Meaning*, 177–83.

29. Doug Murren, *The Baby Boomerang* (Ventura, Calif.: Regal, 1990), 155.

30. George Gallup, Jr., *The Unchurched American. . .10 Years Later*, 26.

31. Doug Murren, *The Baby Boomerang*, 157.

32. David W. Smith, *Men Without Friends* (Nashville: Thomas Nelson, 1990), 55.

33. Daniel Levinson, et al., *The Seasons of a Man's Life* (New York: Alfred A. Knopf, 1978), 335.

34. David W. Smith, *Men Without Friends*, 24–31.

35. Charles Swindoll, *Dropping Your Guard* (Dallas: Word, 1983), 20–21.

36. 1 Samuel 18:1

37. 1 Timothy 1:2

38. Proverbs 18:24

39. David W. Smith, *Men Without Friends*, 31.

40. Galatians 6:2

41. Gary Inrig, *Quality Friendships* (Chicago: Moody Press, 1981), 19.

CHAPTER 5

1. James Patterson and Peter Kim, *The Day America Told the Truth*, 216.

2. Ibid., 5.

3. Matthew 20:28

4. John Haggai, *Lead On!* (Dallas: Word, 1986), 71.

5. Lyle E. Schaller, *It's a Different World* (Nashville: Abingdon Press, 1987), 26–27.

6. George Barna, *The Frog in the Kettle*, 143.

7. George Barna, *The Barna Report, 1992–1993*, 190–93.

8. Roy O'Connor, "Apple Chief Sculley Finally Making the Company His Own," *The Chicago Tribune*, June 1, 1991, sec. 4, 1.

9. James Patterson and Peter Kim, *The Day America Told the Truth*, 230.

10. Ibid., 236.

11. George Barna, *Never On A Sunday*, 24.

12. George Gallup, Jr. and Jim Castelli, *The People's Religion*, 146.

13. Doug Murren, *The Baby Boomerang*, 54. Emphasis in original.

14. Gary R. Collins and Timothy E. Clinton, *Baby Boomer Blues*, 99.

15. Associated Press dispatch, "Church Lacks Hold Over Baby Boomers," *The Chicago Tribune*, June 5, 1992, sec. 2, 7.

16. "Here Come the Baby Boomers," *Emerging Trends*, June 1991, 5.

17. George Gallup, Jr., *The Unchurched American . . . 10 Years Later*, 36.

18. George Barna, *The Frog in the Kettle*, 119.

19. George Gallup, Jr., *The Unchurched American . . . 10 Years Later*, 8.

20. George Barna, *What Americans Believe* (Ventura, Calif.: Regal, 1991), 280.

21. "Making Sense of the Men's Movement," *Focus on the Family*, June 1992, 4.

22. "The Promise Keepers," *Focus on the Family*, June 1992, 4.

23. Jim Dethmer, "What is a Man?" (South Barrington, Ill.: Seeds Tape Ministry, 1991), Tape C9117.

24. Mike Yorkey and Peb Jackson, "Finding New Friends on the Block," *Focus on the Family*, June 1992, 3.

25. Galatians 3:28

26. Gilbert Bilezikian, *Beyond Sex Roles* (Grand Rapids, Mich.: Baker, 1985).

27. John 14:6

28. Drew Kampion and Phil Catalfo, "All In The Family: What Do You Tell Your Children About Faith, Spirit, And The Meaning Of Life," *New Age Journal*, July/August 1992, 54–59.

29. George Barna, *Never On A Sunday*, 16.

30. R. C. Sproul, *Reason to Believe* (Grand Rapids, Mich.: Lamplighter, 1982), 35–36.

31. George Barna, *The Frog in the Kettle*, 137.

32. George Barna, *Never On A Sunday*, 3.

33. Gary L. Collins and Timothy E. Clinton, *Baby Boomer Blues*, 74.

34. "The Case of the Missing Boomers," *Ministry Currents*, January–March 1992, 1.

35. George Barna, *The Barna Report, 1992–93*, 92, 94.

CHAPTER 6

1. This account is based on a story reported by Larry Mueller in "Heroes for Today; The Man and the Mountain Lion," *Reader's Digest*, January 1989, 108–09. His article was originally published in *Outdoor Life*, December 1986.

2. John 4:1–6

3. Matthew 11:19

4. John 4:7–9

5. John 4:10–15

6. See John 4:25, 26

7. See John 4:16–19

8. See John 1:43–50

9. See John 2:1–11

10. See John 2:23

11. Matthew 11:4, 5

12. Lee Strobel and Bill Hybels, "The Case for Christ" (South Barrington, Ill.: Seeds Tape Ministries, 1992), Tape Album AM9215.

13. 1 Peter 3:15b

14. Luke 9:20b

15. Some introductory resources: Cliffe Knechtle, *Give Me an Answer* (Downers Grove, Ill.: InterVarsity Press, 1986); Paul Little, *Know Why You Believe* (Downers Grove, Ill.: InterVarsity Press, 1988; revised and updated edition); Norman Geisler and Ron Brooks, *When Skeptics Ask: a Handbook on Christian Evidences* (Wheaton, Ill.: Victor Books, 1990); Josh McDowell, *More Than a Carpenter* (Wheaton, Ill.: Living Books, 1977); R.C. Sproul, *Reason to Believe* (Grand Rapids, Mich.: Lamplighter, 1978); D. James Kennedy, *Why I Believe* (Dallas: Word, 1980).

16. Paul Little, *How To Give Away Your Faith* (Downers Grove, Ill.: InterVarsity Press, 1988, expanded and updated edition), 109–27

17. John 4:28–30

18. George Barna, *What Americans Believe* (Ventura, Calif.: Regal, 1991), 274.

19. John 4:35

20. John 4:39

21. John 4:41

22. John 4:32–34

CHAPTER 7

1. See Deuteronomy 4:29; Proverbs 8:17; Jeremiah 29:13; Matthew 7:7, 8; Luke 11:10; Hebrews 11:6.

2. American Scientific Affiliation, *Modern Science and Christian Faith* (Wheaton, Ill.: Van Kampen, 1945).

3. Irwin H. Linton, *A Lawyer Examines the Bible* (Grand Rapids, Mich.: Baker, 1943).

4. Viggo Olsen, *The Agnostic Who Dared to Search* (Chicago: Moody Press, 1990).

5. See Bob Chuvala, "A Russian Atheist Finds Jesus," *The Christian Herald* (November/December 1991), 27.

6. Luke 19:10

7. 2 Peter 3:9

8. Paul C. Vitz, "The Psychology of Atheism" (*Truth: An International, Inter-disciplinary Journal of Christian Thought*; Volume 1, 1958), 29.

9. William J. Murray, *My Life Without God* (Nashville: Nelson, 1982), 8.

10. William J. Murray, *The Church Is Not For Perfect People* (Eugene, Ore.: Harvest House, 1987), 36.

11. John Guest, *In Search of Certainty* (Ventura, Calif.: Regal, 1983), 49.

12. Ibid., 51.

13. Cliffe Knechtle, *Give Me an Answer* (Downers Grove, Ill.: InterVarsity Press, 1986), 88–89.

14. Aldous Huxley, *Ends and Means* (London: Chatto & Windus, 1969), 270, 273.
15. Romans 10:13
16. George Barna, *The Church Today* (Glendale, Calif.: Barna Research Group, 1990), 11.
17. Emphasis added. I adapted this approach from remarks about John 1:12 in some unpublished papers of Paul Little. My thanks to his widow, Marie Little, for allowing me to peruse them, as well as for her friendship and partnership in evangelism.
18. 2 Corinthians 5:17
19. Mark 2:17

CHAPTER 8

1. Eugene Peterson, *Traveling Light* (Downers Grove, Ill.: InterVarsity Press, 1982), 45.
2. John 15:13
3. Philippians 4:6
4. Larry Kayser and Rob Wilkins, "A Wing and a Prayer" (South Barrington, Ill.: Seeds Tape Ministry, 1989), Tape C8915, contains an account of the hijacking.
5. Gary Collins, *You Can Make a Difference* (Grand Rapids, Mich.: Zondervan, 1992), 252.
6. James 4:17
7. See Judges 6:15
8. Judges 6:12
9. Collins, *You Can Make a Difference*, 16.
10. See 1 Corinthians 12:7
11. Tim Hansel, *Holy Sweat* (Dallas: Word, 1987), 73.

CHAPTER 9

1. 2 Corinthians 6:14
2. Ecclesiastes 4:9, 10
3. 1 Peter 3:15
4. See 1 Peter 3:1–2
5. Jo Berry, *Beloved Unbeliever* (Grand Rapids, Mich.: Zondervan, 1981), 58.
6. Ezekiel 36:26
7. See Victor Goertzel and Mildred George Goertzel, *Cradles of Eminence* (Boston: Little, Brown, 1962).
8. Romans 5:3–5

CHAPTER 10

1. 1 Corinthians 9:22

2. For a helpful discussion of this distinction, see Millard Erickson, *Christian Theology* (Grand Rapids, Mich.: Baker, 1985) 112–20.

3. Matthew 28:19–20

4. Jim Dethmer, *Seeker-Sensitive or Seeker-Targeted?* (South Barrington, Ill.: Seeds Tape Ministry, 1992), Tape CL850.

5. Doug Murren, *The Baby Boomerang*, 191.

6. George Gallup, Jr., *The Unchurched American . . . 10 Years Later*, 27.

7. Dethmer, *Seeker-Sensitive or Seeker-Targeted?*

8. George G. Hunter III, *How To Reach Secular People* (Nashville: Abingdon Press, 1992), 155.

9. Dethmer, *Seeker-Sensitive or Seeker-Targeted?*

10. Murren, *The Baby Boomerang*, 39, 191.

11. Bill Hybels, *Seven-Step Philosophy* (South Barrington, Ill.: Seeds Tape Ministry, 1990), Tape C9002.

12. Ibid.

13. *Can This Be a Church?* (Troy, Mich.: Kensington Community Church, 1991), 2.

14. From telephone interview with Rev. Trevor Waldock, the Waterfront Church, Southampton, England, Sept. 22, 1992.

15. Colossians 4:5

CHAPTER 11

1. George Barna, *Never On A Sunday*, 34.

2. Ibid.

3. Ibid.

4. Ibid., 26.

CHAPTER 12

1. Franky Schaeffer, *Addicted to Mediocrity* (Westchester, Ill.: Crossway, 1981), 11.

2. Doug Murren, *The Baby Boomerang*, 188.

CHAPTER 13

1. Peter Brierley, *"Christian" England: What the English Church Census Reveals* (London: MARC Europe, 1991), 22 and 59.

2. Ibid, 47. The average attendance at a Protestant church in England is fewer than seventy-five people.

3. See Martin Robinson, *A World Apart: Creating a Church for the Unchurched* (Tunbridge Wells, England: Monarch, 1992), 157–69, for an account of how the Waterfront Church started.

4. See Malachi 1:14

5. Franky Schaeffer, *Addicted to Mediocrity* (Westchester, Ill.: Crossway, 1981), 45. Also see H. R. Rookmaaker, *Art Needs No*

Justification (Downers Grove, Ill.: InterVarsity Press, 1981) and Leland Ryken, editor, *The Christian Imagination* (Grand Rapids, Mich.: Baker, 1985).

6. Nancy Beach, "A Passion for Excellence," *Willow Creek*, July/August 1991, 30.

7. Genesis 1:31

8. From *Roots*, a pamphlet published by the Baptist Union of Great Britain, 1992.

9. Ibid.

10. Thomas J. Peters and Robert H. Waterman, Jr., *In Search of Excellence: Lessons from America's Best-Run Companies* (New York: Harper & Row, 1982).

CHAPTER 14

1. James Patterson and Peter Kim, *The Day America Told the Truth* (New York: Prentice Hall, 1991), 143.

2. "No Comment Department," *Christianity Today*, October 5, 1992, 19.

3. "Clergy Abuse," *USA Today*, October 19, 1992, 3A.

4. Michael Hirsley, "Silence Is Broken: Victims of Sexual Abuse by Clergy Seek Strength and Answers at Conference," *The Chicago Tribune*, October 19, 1992, sec. 2, 1.

5. R. C. Sproul, *Reason to Believe* (Grand Rapids, Mich.: Lamplighter, 1982), 83–84.

6. Warren W. Wiersbe, *The Integrity Crisis* (Nashville: Oliver Nelson, 1988), 21.

7. George H. Gallup, Jr. and Timothy K. Jones, *The Saints Among Us* (Ridgefield, Conn.: Moorehouse, 1992), 13.

8. David McCasland with Roy Irving, "The Education of a Doubter," *Power for Living*, July/August, 1991, 7.

9. William J. Murray, *The Church Is Not For Perfect People* (Eugene, Ore.: Harvest House, 1987), 45–46.

10. See Romans 3:23

11. R. C. Sproul, *Reason To Believe*, 79.

12. George Gallup, Jr. and Jim Castelli, *The People's Religion: American Faith in the '90s*, 144.

13. George Barna, *Never On A Sunday: The Challenge of the Unchurched*, 14.

14. See Barbara Dolan, "Full House At Willow Creek: A Multimedia Appeal to the 'Unchurched Harrys,'" *TIME*, March 6, 1989, 60.

15. Warren Wiersbe, *The Integrity Crisis*, 105.

CHAPTER 15

1. George Barna, *Never On A Sunday*, 24–25.

2. Ibid., 28.

3. Bill Hybels, "Speaking to the Secular Mind," *Leadership/88*, summer quarter, 1988, 31.

4. Psalms 34:8

5. Alan Walker, *The Whole Gospel for the Whole World* (Nashville: Abingdon, 1957), 59.

6. Bill Hybels, "Speaking to the Secular Mind," 30.

7. 1 Corinthians 13:1–2

CHAPTER 16

1. Luke 15:10

2. See Luke 24:47

3. Psalm 40:1–3, *New Century Version*.

Willow Creek Association

Vision, Training, Resources for Prevailing Churches

This resource was created to serve you and to help you in building a local church that prevails!

Since 1992, the Willow Creek Association (WCA) has been linking like-minded, action-oriented churches with each other and with strategic vision, training, and resources. Now a worldwide network of over 6,400 churches from more than ninety denominations, the WCA works to equip Member Churches and others with the tools needed to build prevailing churches. Our desire is to inspire, equip, and encourage Christian leaders to build biblically functioning churches that reach increasing numbers of unchurched people, not just with innovations from Willow Creek Community Church in South Barrington, Illinois, but from any church in the world that has experienced God-given breakthroughs.

WILLOW CREEK CONFERENCES

Each year, thousands of local church leaders, staff and volunteers—from WCA Member Churches and others—attend one of our conferences or training events. Conferences offered on the Willow Creek campus in South Barrington, Illinois, include:

Prevailing Church Conference: Foundational training for staff and volunteers working to build a prevailing local church.

Prevailing Church Workshops: More than fifty strategic, day-long workshops covering seven topic areas that represent key characteristics of a prevailing church; offered twice each year.

Promiseland Conference: Children's ministries; infant through fifth grade.

Student Ministries Conference: Junior and senior high ministries.

Willow Creek Arts Conference: Vision and training for Christian artists using their gifts in the ministries of local churches.

Leadership Summit: Envisioning and equipping Christians with leadership gifts and responsibilities; broadcast live via satellite to eighteen cities across North America.

Contagious Evangelism Conference: Encouragement and training for churches and church leaders who want to be strategic in reaching lost people for Christ.

Small Groups Conference: Exploring how developing a church *of* small groups can play a vital role in developing authentic Christian community that leads to spiritual transformation.

To find out more about WCA conferences, visit our website at www.willowcreek.com.

PREVAILING CHURCH REGIONAL WORKSHOPS

Each year the WCA team leads several, two-day training events in select cities across the United States. Some twenty day-long workshops are offered in topic areas including leadership, next-generation ministries, small groups, arts and worship, evangelism, spiritual gifts, financial stewardship, and spiritual formation. These events make quality training more accessible and affordable to larger groups of staff and volunteers.

To find out more about Prevailing Church Regional Workshops, visit our website at www.willowcreek.com.

WILLOW CREEK RESOURCES™

Churches can look to Willow Creek Resources™ for a trusted channel of ministry tools in areas of leadership, evangelism, spiritual gifts, small groups, drama, contemporary music, financial stewardship, spiritual transformation, and more. For ordering information, call (800) 570-9812 or visit our website at www.willowcreek.com.

WCA MEMBERSHIP

Membership in the Willow Creek Association as well as attendance at WCA Conferences is for churches, ministries, and leaders who hold to a historic, orthodox understanding of biblical Christianity. The annual church membership fee of $249 provides substantial discounts for your entire team on all conferences and Willow Creek Resources, networking opportunities with other outreach-oriented churches, a bimonthly newsletter, a subscription to the *Defining Moments* monthly audio journal for leaders, and more.

To find out more about WCA membership, visit our website at www.willowcreek.com.

WILLOWNET (WWW.WILLOWCREEK.COM)

This Internet resource service provides access to hundreds of Willow Creek messages, drama scripts, songs, videos, and multimedia ideas. The system allows you to sort through these elements and download them for a fee.

Our website also provides detailed information on the Willow Creek Association, Willow Creek Community Church, WCA membership, conferences, training events, resources, and more.

WILLOWCHARTS.COM (WWW.WILLOWCHARTS.COM)

Designed for local church worship leaders and musicians, WillowCharts.com provides online access to hundreds of music charts and chart components, including choir, orchestral, and horn sections, as well as rehearsal tracks and video streaming of Willow Creek Community Church performances.

THE NET (HTTP://STUDENTMINISTRY.WILLOWCREEK.COM)

The NET is an online training and resource center designed by and for student ministry leaders. It provides an inside look at the structure, vision, and mission of prevailing student ministries from around the world. The NET gives leaders access to complete programming elements, including message outlines, dramas, small group questions, and more. An indispensable resource and networking tool for prevailing student ministry leaders!

CONTACT THE WILLOW CREEK ASSOCIATION

If you have comments or questions, or would like to find out more about WCA events or resources, please contact us:

Willow Creek Association
P.O. Box 3188, Barrington, IL 60011-3188
Phone: (800) 570-9812 or (847) 765-0070
Fax (888) 922-0035 or (847) 765-5046
Web: www.willowcreek.com

Resources by Lee Strobel

The Case for Christ

The Case for Christ Audio Pages®

The Case for Christ—Student Edition (with Jane Vogel)

The Case for Faith

The Case for Faith Audio Pages®

The Case for Faith—Student Edition (with Jane Vogel)

God's Outrageous Claims

Surviving a Spiritual Mismatch in Marriage
(with Leslie Strobel)

Surviving a Spiritual Mismatch in Marriage Audio
Pages®

What Jesus Would Say

We want to hear from you. Please send your comments about this book to us in care of the address below. Thank you.

ZONDERVAN™

GRAND RAPIDS, MICHIGAN 49530 USA

WWW.ZONDERVAN.COM